QSE
QUICK SMART ENGLISH

Pre-Intermediate A2-B1

Rebecca Robb Benne

with

Joanne Collie

BROOKEMEAD ENGLISH
LANGUAGE TEACHING

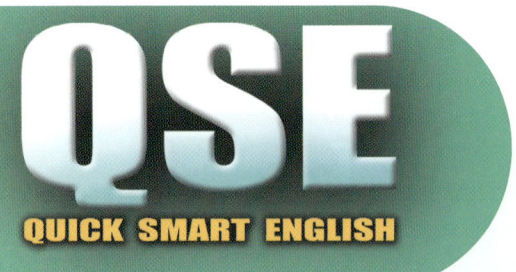

QSE
QUICK SMART ENGLISH

Pre-Intermediate A2-B1

Series editor: Duncan Prowse
Contributor and consultant: Joanne Collie
Consultant: Rosemary Harris
Assistant editors: Deborah Friedland, Anna Kutz
Designer: John Anastasio
Research and permissions: Veena Holkar, Pupak Navabpour
Artists: Cedric Knight, Mark Duffin
Glossary: Mary Rigby
Recordings: John Green, Tim Woolf

QSE Pre-Intermediate
Common European Framework Level A2-B1

Student's book: **ISBN 978-1-905248-08-7**

Also available:
QSE Pre-Intermediate Workbook, ISBN 978-1-905248-09-4
QSE Pre-Intermediate CD 1 Listening and pronunciation, ISBN 978-1-905248-10-0
QSE Pre-Intermediate CD 2 Reading, ISBN 978-1-905248-11-7
QSE Pre-Intermediate Teacher's Guide, ISBN 978-1-905248-15-5

Other books in the QSE Series:
QSE Intermediate (CEF B1-B2)
Student's Book, Workbook, Audio CDs, Teacher's Guide
QSE Advanced (CEF B2-C1)
Student's Book and Workbook, Video and Audio on DVD or CD, Teacher's Guide

Produced and published by:
Brookemead English Language Teaching, London

Acknowledgements

Cover: top:Comstock/Alamy, middle left: A1PIX/Sunset, middle:Picture courtesy of www.tandemfreefall.co.uk, bottom © Salamander Photo. **Unit 1:** p8l: image100/Alamy; p8tr: Paul Springett/Alamy; p8mr: Brand X Pictures/Alamy; p9tr Everett Collection/Rex Features; p9ml:image 100/alamy; p9mr A1PIX; p9br:Brand X Pictures/Alamy; p10:Picture courtesy of www.tandemfreefall.co.uk; p11: Stockbyte Platinum/Alamy. **Unit 2:** p12tr, br; p13:Photos by Silviano courtesy of www.ipanema.com; p14tr:©Timothy N. Holt 2003 www.phatfotos.com; p14bl:Giles Moberly/Alamy; p15tl:Create Music Ltd – 01782 267845. **Unit 3:** p16tr: Roger Ball/CORBIS p16mr:Crystal Ski; p16br:Tom Bible/Alamy; p17ml:Crystal Ski; p17m: Thomson Holidays 2005; p17mr: Worldwide Picture Library/Alamy; p18l:Image source/Alamy; p18r:Bob Thomas/Getty Images p19t:2005 Microsoft Corporation; p19ml:© 2005 SMART Technologies Inc. Used with permission. **Unit 4:** p20t: PETER BROOKER/Rex Features; p20m:Richard T. Nowitz/CORBIS; p20b: Moviestore Collection Ltd; p21l:Bill Davila/rex Features/REX FEATURES; p20r:Starstock/Photoshot; p22l,r:© ABC Photography Archives/2005 ABC Inc.p23:© www.moviemistakes.com. **Unit 5:** p24a: Royalty-free/Corbis; p24b:APACS; p24c:Eyebyte/Alamy; p24d:© Boots; p24e:Photo provided by Body Mechanics Inc. © Copyright 2005 Body Mechanics, Inc. All rights reserved. For more information on Backpack Safety International TM, visit www.backpacksafe.com, write to info@backpacksafe.com or call 00-1-843-881-4631; p24f:APACS; p24g:Royalty-free/Corbis,24h:Joe Tree/Alamy; p25l:Image Source/Alamy; p25m:Editorial Partners,Tokyo; p24r:Brand X Pictures/Alamy; p26l:BananaStock / Alamy; p26r:Editorial Partners,Tokyo; p27tl: Dynamic Graphics Group/IT Stock Free/Alamy; p27tr:Crown Copyright material reproduced with the permission of Queen's Printer and Controller of Her Majesty's Stationery Office [Licence C02W0006000]. **Unit 6:** p28:Duncan Prowse; p29tr:Compassion In World Farming www.ciwf.org; p29mr:Wayne Lawler; Ecoscene/CORBIS; p30:BananaStock/Alamy; p31:U.S. Department of Agriculture and U.S. Department of Health and Human Services. **Unit 7:** p32tm:ALG187187 Head of Mary Magdalene Crying, from the Crucifixion (fresco) by Ercole de Roberti (c.1453-96) Pinacoteca Nazionale, Bologna, Italy/Bridgeman Art Library; p32tr:Copyright © Nokia,p32m:Inmagine/Alamy; p32mr:Pink Dancer (pastel) by Degas, Edgar (1834-1917) Private Collection Lefevre Fine Art Ltd., London French, out of copyright/Bridgeman Art Library; p33tl:Salamander Photo; p33tr:Mary Evans Picture Library; p34l:ImageState Royalty Free/Alamy; p34r:Design Pics Inc./Alamy; p35l:BananaStock/Alamy; p35r:© The artist, Giancarlo Neri / ROLLO Contemporary Art. **Unit 8:** p36tr,m:©2005 Kjeld Duits/iKjeld.com; p36mr:Police 2005 advertising campaign featuring David Beckham; p37:Editorial Partners,Tokyo, 38l:Photo Jane Dallaway; p38m,r: Nokia (Copyright© Nokia); p39tr:EMPICS/AP; p39m:david sanger photography/Alamy. **Ext Read 1:** p40:Vincent Curutchet/DPPI/Offshore Challenges; p41: Rex Features. TEXT p41: Reprinted by kind permission of *Spiegel* and Ellen MacArthur. **Unit 9:** p42t:Don Tremain / Alamy; p42m:Steve Allen / Alamy; p42b:David Stares/Alamy; p43:© JP Laffont/Sygma/CORBIS; p44t:© Earl & Nazima Kowall/CORBIS; p44m:Comstock Images / Alamy; p44b:David Hoffman Photo Library/Alamy; p45l:Photo European Parliament; p45m: Photo European Parliament – Architecte: Association des architectes du CIC: Vanden Bossche sprl, C.R.V s.a., CDG sprl, Studiegroep D. Bontinck; p45r:Source BBC. **Unit 10:** p46tl:© The Trustees of The British Museum; p46tr:Mary Evans Picture Library; p46mr:MARY EVANS/THOMAS GILLMOR COLLECTION; p47:Reproduced by permission of Hodder and Stoughton Limited; p47 TEXT:EAGER by Helen Fox. Reproduced by permission of Hodder and Stoughton Limited; p48t:Image of Viera 42PE50B courtesy of Panasonic; p48m: © Dyson, 48b:Image of DVD S97 courtesy of Panasonic; p49l:© Sony Corporation; p49tr:Honda (UK). **Unit 11:** p50t:EMPICS/AP; p50m:P&O Ferries; p50b:© Honda; p51tr:Steve Hamblin/Alamy; p51ml:Dirk v. Mallinckrodt/Alamy; p52l:HIE/Stockscotland.com; p52r:J. Broadhurst/Stockscotland.com. **Unit 12:** p54tr:David Hoffman Photo Library/Alamy; p54bm,br:Image Source/Alamy; p55tl:Mark Dyball/Alamy; p55mr:Image Source/Alamy; p56:Design Pics Inc./Alamy; p57tl: John Foxx/Alamy; p57ml: Anon/DHD Multimedia Gallery; p57bl,br: picturesbyrob/ Alamy. **Unit 13:** p58tr:© Rob Titherley; p58ml:Henry Iddon - www.fineline.ph; p59t:Carphotos/Alamy; p59m:Rex Features, 60tl:Brand X Pictures/Alamy; p60tr:Karl Weatherly/Getty Images; p61t, ml:AP/EMPICS; p61bl: © PhysicsCentral.com. **Unit 14:** p63l:image100/Alamy; p63r:Photography by Steve Young of dreamweddingshawaii.com; p64l:Dynamic Graphics Group/Creatas/Alamy; p64r:© Jose Luis Pelaez, Inc./CORBIS. p65: Mark Duffin. **Unit 15:** p66a:ImageState Royalty Free/Alamy; p66b:freeimages.co.uk; p66c:Comstock Images/Alamy; p66d:John Foxx/Alamy; p66e:freeimages.co.uk; p67:AFP/Getty Images; p68:FREDERIC J. BROWN/AFP/Getty Images; p69tr,mr: Reprinted with permission ©2005 American Lung Association. For more information about the American Lung Association or to support the work it does, call 1-800-LUNG-USA (1-800-586-4872) or log on to www.lungusa.org. **Unit 16:** p70t:A1PIX/Sunset; p70m:geogphotos/Alamy; p70b:StockShot/Alamy; p70tl:A1PIX/Sunset; p71ml:A1PIX; p72:Photodisc/Getty Images. **Ext Read 2:** p74:© Mark Rusher; p75: Cover photograph – Michael Wildsmith, TEXT p75: © (abridged) Benjamin Zephaniah/Bloomsbury Publishing 1999.

Every effort has been made to trace and acknowledge the copyright holders of all material used in this book. The publishers apologise for any omissions and will be pleased to make necessary arrangements when this book is reprinted.

QSE Pre-Intermediate

Unit	Title	Subject	The BIG question	Functions, Language Banks	Grammar
1	**Adrenalin rush**	Hobbies and sports, holidays	*Do we need danger?*	1 Talking about permanent situations and repeated actions 2 Talking about the past and sequencing events	The past simple/ present simple, sequencing words
2	**Carnival atmosphere**	Festivals and music	*Why are we celebrating?*	3 Giving advice (*should*) 4 Describing frequency and manner	Adverbs of frequency and manner
3	**Lifestyle choices**	Work, job satisfaction	*What kind of job is best for you?*	5 Comparing two things, more than two things	Comparatives, superlatives of adjectives
4	**Stranger than fiction**	Entertainment	*Are reality shows good TV?*	6 Expressing likes and dislikes 7 Talking about future plans and intentions	*Going to* future
5	**Shopaholics**	Shops and shopping	*Do shops rip you off?*	8 Complaining 9 Quantifying	Adverbials of quantity
6	**Eat your greens!**	Food	*Must we kill to eat?*	10 Asking for and giving reasons 11 Making and replying to requests	Connecting words: *and, but, because*
7	**For your eyes only**	Diaries, blogs	*What do you keep private?*	12 Talking about events in the indefinite or recent past	Present perfect with *ever, never, just*
8	**Fashionistas**	Fashion	*Are you a fashion leader?*	13 Talking on the phone 14 Expressing preferences	Articles
	Extended reading 1	Fame and success			

Quick Smart English   Pre-Intermediate   CONTENTS

QSE Pre-Intermediate

Quick Smart English   Pre-Intermediate   CONTENTS

Evaluation sheets x 2 – for LLE
Plane times (Planning & for Paperwork stay)
Diaries
Copy diary entries
Projects + photocopying?
1 Last lesson?
Shopping & thank Yous
Pub – Text Botwha?   Shopping
Indian meal –
RUTH K
ALISON?
ANDREW MAXWELL
Check emails
David
Bamford

Adrenalin rush

1 *The BIG question:*

DO WE NEED DANGER?

FACT: Every year in the USA, over 700,000 young people go to hospital because of sporting injuries. Most injuries are from traditional sports like football.

2 FOCUS ON ...

Words

A 1 Put the words and phrases below into one of these categories.

(a) Traditional sports ....

(b) Extreme sports ....

baseball   BMX biking   skydiving   football (UK) / soccer (US)
inline skating   surfing   cuts and bruises   swimming
sprained wrist/knee   broken bone   basketball   cracked rib
bungee jumping   tennis

  2 Can you add other words? Use a dictionary.

(c) Sporting injuries

....

B Match each sentence with its opposite meaning.

1 It's safe.
2 It's boring.
3 I avoided injuries.
4 I hated it.
5 I'm worried.

a) I'm relaxed.
b) I loved it.
c) It gives me an adrenalin rush.
d) It's dangerous.
e) I got hurt.

C These sentences are in the interviews on the page opposite.
Which sentences are about:
1 a reason for doing an extreme sport?
2 a problem in an extreme sport?

- I cracked a rib.
- I want to show that girls can do anything.
- I love the adrenalin rush.

D Work with a partner. Ask and answer the questions.
1 Which sports are dangerous?
2 Why do people do extreme sports?
3 Do you like danger? Why or why not?

Ideas

Discuss these statements with a partner:
A Parents must stop their children doing an extreme sport.
B I admire people who do dangerous sports.

3 READING

A Read the interviews quickly. Match each interview to a picture.

1 I started racing BMX bikes at five. My parents hated it so, at 16, I did other sports like tennis and football. But I loved danger. I finally went back to biking at 20. When I started, I had lots of injuries. I had broken bones, cuts and bruises and I cracked a rib. Then I learnt how to fall and how to avoid injury. I love the adrenalin rush – there's nothing like that feeling.

5

2 First, my parents gave me a pair of roller skates. Then they saved up to buy me inline skates. At 16, I started competing. I just loved the sport. I hate it when guys say girls can't do things – that's what pushes me to be better. I want to show that girls can do anything they want to. But then I got a sprained knee. That injury usually takes about six weeks to get better.

10

15

3 I started at 20, four years ago. It's really the sport for me. The thrill of danger stops time and makes every colour seem brighter. In the air, I really feel alive! The adrenalin rush is so exciting, you just don't know until you try. It stays with you for life. I'm lucky, I never get any injuries. My mom doesn't like it at all. She comes to shows but she never watches me jump.

20

4 I first tried surfing in Australia, when I was 15. My parents were worried. They thought surfing was dangerous. For me, danger was thrilling! When I got home, I started riding waves every day at a beach near my house. My parents finally agreed that surfing was OK for girls. Now they find it exciting, too. Everyone growing up wants to do things. If you do something you love, that's when you're a happy person.

25

a) Paula Carrera, surfer

b) Gary Lansdowne, BMX biker

c) Francine O'Reilly, inline skater

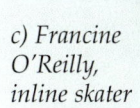

d) Juan Julia, skydiver

B Read the interviews again.
1 Answer the questions for each person.
   a) When did you start your sport?
   b) What do your parents think of it?
   c) Do you ever get sports injuries?
   d) Why do you do it?
2 What did Gary Lansdowne do when he was: a) 5   b) 16   c) 20?
3 Write four sentences about Gary, using:
   a) *First*   b) *Then*   c) *Finally*
4 Write sentences like the sentences in 3 for another athlete.

C Compare your ideas with a partner.
1 Which interview did you find most interesting? Why?
2 Which sport do you think is most difficult? Which is most dangerous?
3 What other questions would you like to ask the athletes?

4 LANGUAGE

A Look at the verbs in these sentences.
- I **started** at 20, four years ago.
- I **got** a sprained knee.
- It **stays** with you for life.
- She **comes** to shows but she never **watches** me jump.

Which verb describes something that:
1 is permanent, is there all the time?
2 happened at a specific time in the past?
3 happens (or doesn't happen) many times, like a routine?
4 happened at one specific time, but the time is not mentioned?

B Read the interviews again and find the past forms of these irregular verbs.
- be   - get   - give   - think   - learn

WORKBOOK UNIT 1: THE PRESENT SIMPLE AND PAST SIMPLE

Adrenalin rush

First jump: the student and instructor jump together

 5   LISTEN IN

A Before you listen, answer the questions.
1   What kinds of injuries do sports players have?
2   What can you do to protect yourself from injury when you play sports?

B Listen to two young people talking about sports. What sport does each one like?
1   Alicia likes …..
2   Tim likes …..

C Put the arguments in the correct column.

What Alicia says about extreme sports	What Tim says about traditional sports

1   It gives you a great feeling.
2   You're scared, but you do it anyway.
3   You work with others in a team.
4   You do things by yourself.
5   It's good exercise.
6   The danger is thrilling.
7   You're with friends.
8   It's safe.

D Work with a partner. Listen again. Write arguments AGAINST extreme sports and AGAINST traditional sports.

6   YOUR TURN TO SPEAK

A Role play
Use the ideas in 5C and 5D and **Language Bank 1**. Choose an extreme sport. Take turns to be the student and the teacher. The student persuades the teacher that it's a good idea for the school to give lessons in the extreme sport.

B Conversation
Use **Language Bank 2**. Work with a partner. Tell her / him about a time when you, or someone you know, was in danger or injured.
1   What happened first? Then what happened? Finally, what was the result?
2   What was the reaction of others, for example parents or friends?
3   What lessons did you, or the person you know, learn from the event?

7   YOUR TOPIC

Choose a sport that you like. Make notes about:
• Good things about it
• Possible dangers
• Things you have to learn to do it well
• Things you do or wear to be safe
Tell your group or the class about your sport. Answer their questions. Use **Language Bank 1** to help you.

FIRST AID ➕ *in English*

Why not quiz the coach? The coach gives great advice!

Dear Coach,
I went skateboarding and fell on my knee. It really hurts. What can I do?

Boardster, 18

Dear Boardster,
Most injuries happen because the athletes wore NO protection! So, don't forget your knee pads and wrist guards! For now, R.I.C.E. is the answer.
R - REST. Stay off the knee as much as possible.
I - ICE. Put ice around the knee to stop it swelling up.
C - COMPRESS. Put a bandage around the knee to support it.
E - ELEVATE. Lie down, put your leg high up on a cushion.

Hi Coach,
I was inline skating with my friend when she fell and sprained her ankle really badly. Please tell me what to do if it ever happens again.

Lynn, 17

Dear Lynn,
First, don't panic. Here are some First Aid tips for sports injuries:
1 *Help your friend to sit down.*
2 *Remember R.I.C.E.*
3 *Use your mobile phone to ring Emergency Services.*
4 *Say where you are and what the problem is. Ask for an ambulance.*
5 *Keep your friend warm.*

Sprained ankle

A Find words and phrases in the text which mean:
1 something that protects your wrist
2 don't stand on it
3 something cold to put on an injury
4 something soft to put under your leg
5 a car that takes you to hospital
6 a number to ring if there's an accident

B Read the letters again. Put ✅ for things to do and 😣 for things to avoid if someone has an injury.
1 panic
2 ring for an ambulance
3 put ice on a sprained knee
4 keep an injured person warm
5 walk with a sprained knee
6 bandage an injured leg

9 PORTFOLIO WRITING

Write an email to a friend (70–80 words). Tell him or her about a sport experience that you had. Did you enjoy it? Why or why not? Was it dangerous? Did you get injured?

10 *Your answer:* DO WE NEED DANGER?

Are extreme sports thrilling or just scary? Are traditional sports boring? Are all sports dangerous?

 SEE WORKBOOK UNIT 1

Last word:

Can you use all the language items below? Write *Yes*, *No*, or *Almost* against each.

Functions: Talking about permanent situations or repeated actions; talking about the past and sequencing

Language: The present simple, the past simple, and sequencing words

Vocabulary: Extreme sports; injuries; first aid

Subject:	Festivals and music
Functions:	Giving advice; describing frequency and manner
Language:	Adverbs of frequency; adverbs of manner

1 *The BIG question:*

WHY ARE WE CELEBRATING?

 **FACT:** Carnivals aren't just festivals, they're big business. London's Notting Hill Carnival brings in £93m and Rio de Janeiro's Carnival $140 million.

2 FOCUS ON ...

Words

A Match the words in the box to the pictures on this page.

1 costume	2 decorations
3 feathers	4 float
	5 parade

B Combine these verbs and nouns to make phrases.

1 to celebrate	a) a costume
2 to watch	b) a parade
3 to wear	c) a team
4 to have	d) a protest
5 to make	e) a festival
6 to support	f) a good time

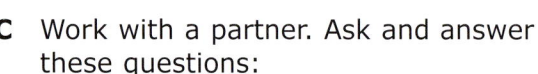

In the Sambódromo in Rio

C Work with a partner. Ask and answer these questions:
1 Do you like parties and festivals? Why or why not?
2 Do you like traditional dress or costumes? Why or why not?
3 What are the main festivals and celebrations in your country?

D Match the words from the text on page 13 with their definitions.

1 sponsorship	a) a person who isn't free
2 a theme	b) causes lots of discussion
3 a slave	c) money for advertising something
4 corrupt	d) a topic
5 a crime	e) selling drugs, for example
6 controversial	f) not honest

Ideas
Discuss these statements with a partner:
A It's good to celebrate the traditions of our country even if we live in a multicultural world.
B I just like a good party. It doesn't matter why we celebrate.

3 READING

A Read the article quickly. What happens at Carnival time in Rio?

A float with the word CENSORED on it. The church often complains about Carnival themes

CELEBRATION OR PROTEST?

The Rio de Janeiro Carnival is a time to drink, dance and celebrate before Lent. As in Catholic Europe, Lent is the forty days before Easter when many Christians stop doing things they enjoy. But the Rio Carnival also includes African dance and music traditions from the ⁵ time when slaves worked on Brazil's coffee plantations.

Millions of people usually watch the street parades all over the city and about 70,000 see the top samba schools in the Sambódromo, Rio's parade street. Rio's samba schools are local social clubs. The ¹⁰ schools choose different themes for every Carnival and members work hard all year to build the floats and make the costumes. Their supporters are proud of them and support them passionately – like their favourite football team. At the samba parade the ¹⁵ schools get points for music, costumes, dancing and enthusiasm.

Slavery, corrupt politicians and crime were Carnival themes in past years and the themes are becoming more controversial each year. Brazil's ²⁰ Roman Catholic Church often complains. In 2004, for example, the church complained about the Acadèmicos da Grande Rio School and its theme of safe sex and AIDS. However, anti-AIDS groups supported the school and protesters gave out free ²⁵ condoms at the Carnival. "Festivals like the Rio Carnival are a good way to teach young people about AIDS," one supporter said. "We're using the Carnival to make a protest," said another.

But a lot of people ask whether protest and ³⁰ education are what the Carnival is really about. Others say that commercial interests such as television rights, tourism and sponsorship are taking over the traditional meaning of Rio's Carnival. Some think it just doesn't matter – what's ³⁵ important is the party.

B Read the text again. Who or what do these sentences refer to?
1 They worked in coffee plantations.
2 They dance in the parade at the Sambódromo.
3 They choose different themes every year.
4 They work hard all year.
5 They are becoming more controversial.
6 It complained.

C Are these sentences about the Rio Carnival true (**T**)? or false (**F**)?　　　　**T/F**
1 There is one parade.　　☐
2 The Carnival takes place before Lent.　　☐
3 The Carnival combines European and African traditions.　　☐
4 It isn't a commercial event.　　☐

D Discuss these questions with a partner.
1 Do you have a carnival in your country? Do you think it's a good tradition?
2 What do you think about commercial sponsorship of festivals?
3 Is it right that particular groups use festivals to promote their ideas?

4 LANGUAGE

Look at the adverbs of frequency and manner in **bold** in these sentences:
- They **usually** watch the parade.
- Members work **hard** all year.
- They support their schools **passionately**.
- They **often** complain.

A Which adverbs answer the question 'How often'? Where do these adverbs go in the sentence?

B Which adverbs answer the question 'How'? Where do they go in the sentence?

C Can you think of other examples of adverbs of frequency and manner?

WORKBOOK UNIT 2: ADVERBS OF FREQUENCY AND MANNER

5 **LISTEN IN**

A Before you listen, look at the pictures. Where do you think this is? What is happening?

B Listen to a reporter at the event in the pictures. Check your ideas from A.

C Read the sentences. Who says them? Listen again and write **M** for the man or **W** for the woman in the interviews.

		W/M
1	Festivals can't survive without sponsorship.	
2	There's often violence and there's alcohol and drugs everywhere.	
3	The organisers don't want to spoil the image of the Carnival.	
4	The food, the floats and costumes are wonderful.	
5	The Carnival's too commercial – but everything's commercial nowadays.	
6	The Carnival makes a lot of money.	
7	The Carnival's too big now.	
8	The music needs to change with the times.	

Notting Hill Carnival, London

6 YOUR TURN TO SPEAK

A **Role play**
Your friend really wants to go to the Notting Hill Carnival. You're worried about the big crowds and violence. Use **Language Bank 3** to give your friend some advice.

B **Conversation**
Work with a partner. Use **Language Bank 4** to talk about the following:
1 How often do you have parties or family celebrations? What do you celebrate?
2 How often do you have special or festival meals? What do you eat?
3 How well can you dance? How often do you dance? Where do you dance?

7 YOUR TOPIC

Choose a festival or celebration in your country. Make notes about:

• Its name, when it happens
• What happens (what people do, eat, wear)
• Its history
• Why you like or don't like it

Present your festival to the class. Answer their questions.

8 MUSIC TECHNOLOGY in English

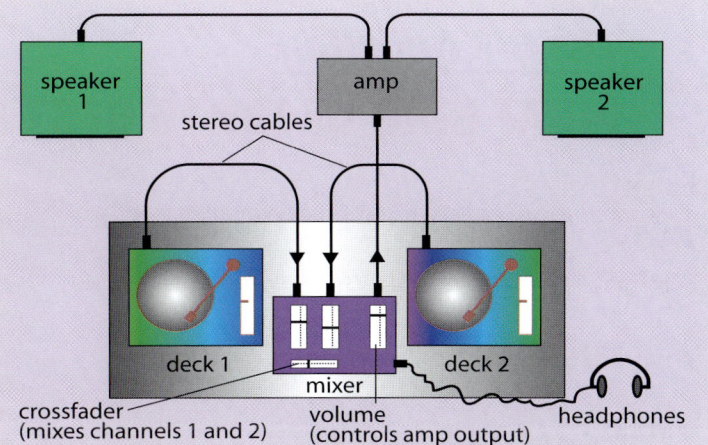

DJ Blakey is UK Champion

DJ mixing is the world's fastest growing music market. Clubbers from Tokyo to Toronto dance to music by famous DJs. DJs use two or more decks (vinyl disc turntables or CD players) to mix together different tracks. A DJ can take the vocal of one track and mix it with the beat of a different track. He or she can also add scratches and other sounds to make new versions of original songs.

9 PORTFOLIO WRITING

Write a profile of your favourite singer or band, or an article about a festival (100–120 words).

10 *Your answer:* WHY ARE WE CELEBRATING?

Is the meaning of festivals changing? Are religious or traditional cultural festivals still more important than modern music festivals?

 SEE WORKBOOK UNIT 2

Last word:

Can you use all the language items below? Write *Yes*, *No*, or *Almost* against each.

Functions: Giving advice; describing frequency and manner

Language: Adverbs of frequency; adverbs of manner

Vocabulary: Festivals; music

A Complete these sentences.
1 DJs mix songs using two ………
2 ……… connect the turntables and the mixer.
3 The ……… makes the music louder.
4 The DJ uses ……… to listen to the tracks.
5 The ……… put the sound into the room.

B Find words in the text which mean:
1 the main rhythm
2 a piece of music on a vinyl disc or CD
3 the singing part
4 the sound when a DJ moves the needle on a vinyl disc

C Discuss these questions with a partner:
1 Do you think mixing is as creative as playing a musical instrument?
2 Do you play any musical instruments?
3 Who are your favourite singers or bands? Why? What do they sing about?
4 Do you go to clubs?

What's new?

Subject:	Work, job satisfaction
Functions:	Comparing
Language:	Comparatives, superlatives

1   *The BIG question:*

WHAT KIND OF JOB IS BEST FOR YOU?

FACT: According to a survey, 43% of people aged 14–19 want to set up their own companies, or work for themselves.

2   FOCUS ON ...

Words

A   Match the people and what they do. Use the pictures in this unit.

1 Computer programmers	a) teach winter sports.
2 Accountants	b) run a business.
3 Garden specialists	c) write software.
4 Managers	d) keep financial records.
5 Ski instructors	e) give advice about plants and sell them.

6    Add other jobs you are interested in. Use a dictionary to add definitions.

B   Find the right endings for these sentences:

1 Sole traders and partnerships are ...	a) riskier than working for a larger company.
2 Large companies are sometimes ...	b) use more creative ideas.
3 A small business lets people ...	c) usually the smallest businesses.
4 Working for a small company is often...	d) stressful places to work.

C   These phrases are in the texts on page 17. Tick ✅ the expressions that mean the best things about a job. Put a cross ❎ for the worst things.

1 Working with people	☐	4 Making lots of money	☐
2 No time for friends	☐	5 A secure job	☐
3 Lots of meetings	☐	6 A challenging job	☐

D   Work with a partner. Ask and answer these questions:
1   Why do many young people want to work for themselves?
2   What is the best (or worst) kind of job for you?

Ideas

Discuss these statements with a partner:

A   Being your own boss is a more secure way of working.

B   It's more challenging to work for a large company.

3 READING

A Read these stories quickly. Choose the best title for each one.

a) **More friends, less money**   b) The most beautiful place in the world   c) Being your own boss

> In a recent survey, over 50% of students agreed that, "Being happy in your job is more important than making lots of money."

1

For Franco Ferrer, 23, the most [1] important thing about a job is working with people. He left his job as a computer programmer in a Milan office to become a ski instructor in the Alps. [5] "I was making more money, but I had less time for friends," he says. "Now I have a smaller flat and [10] no car, but I have never been happier. For me, this is the least stressful lifestyle. [15] Our ski school is a partnership. It's friendlier and healthier in every way than my old job."

2

Adriana Bunti [20] left school at 16 and got a job in a small hotel in Bucharest. [25] She worked as a cleaner, then started helping out at reception. Six [30] years later, she's the hotel manager. But now she wants a more challenging job. "I really want to have my own business," she says. "I want a bigger hotel, and I want to make it the best in [35] the city. Working for yourself is less secure, but being my own boss is the most important thing to me."

3

Gemma Donovan was an accountant in London. Every day, it took her two [40] hours to drive to work. "It was a large company and everyone was stressed," she says. "Too many meetings; I got home late [45] and tired." She moved to New Zealand, trained in a garden centre, and now [50] owns her own small business growing and selling plants. "It's more challenging," she says, "and it's more interesting. I spend most of my time outdoors, in the most [55] beautiful place in the world. What could be better?"

B 1 Read the articles again. Who:

a) cleaned rooms?   b) now lives in a beautiful place?
c) spent a lot of time in a car?   d) now has a friendlier job?
e) made a lot of money?   f) now wants a less secure job?

2 Complete the table with the correct expressions.

	Old job	New job
Franco Ferrer		
Adriana Bunti		
Gemma Donovan		

a) working in a hotel   b) owning a business   c) a more challenging job
d) working for a large company   e) working with computers   f) a healthier lifestyle

C Compare your ideas with a partner.

1 Do the articles conclude that one kind of job is better than another?

2 Which of the jobs do you find most interesting? Why?

4 LANGUAGE

Look at these sentences:
- Being happy is **more important** than making money.
- **The most important** thing is having an interesting job.
- It's **friendlier, healthier,** and **less stressful** than my old job.
- It's **the most beautiful** place in the world.

A Which sentences compare: 1 two things? 2 more than two things?

B Find words that compare two things by adding **-er** to the end of the adjective.

C Find words that compare two things by adding **more** or **less**.

WORKBOOK UNIT 3: COMPARATIVES AND SUPERLATIVES

5 LISTEN IN ③

A Before you listen, look at the pictures.
  1 What jobs are these?
  2 What are the good things about these jobs?
  3 For you, do these phrases have
     positive ➕ or negative ➖ meanings?

- jobs for geeks ☐ • financial analyst ☐
- a good salary ☐ • routine and promotion ☐
- I'm a techie ☐ • freelance reporter ☐

B Listen to Gary and Lynn.
Write **L** for things that Lynn wants, and
G for things that Gary wants.

1 to see other countries	☐
2 to learn new things	☐
3 to work with numbers	☐
4 to use information technology	☐
5 to work with people	☐
6 to have a good salary	☐
7 to have adventures	☐
8 to have more fun	☐

C Work with a partner. Write two lists of
arguments:
  1 for a secure job with a good salary.
  2 for a freelance job with lots of variety
     and adventure.

6 YOUR TURN TO SPEAK

A Role play
  Choose one of the jobs in this unit. Role
  play a discussion between yourself and a
  career adviser. The adviser doesn't think
  this job is right for you. Persuade him /
  her that it's really a great choice.

B Conversation
  Use **Language Bank 5**. Make a list of the
  three most important things for you in your
  career. Work with a partner and talk about
  these questions:
  1 Which is better for you:
     a) working in an office or outdoors?
     b) working with people or computers?
     c) travelling a lot or staying in one
        place and getting to know it?
  2 What is the most important thing in life
     for you? Is it making money?

7 YOUR TOPIC

Choose a job that you would like. Make notes
about:
- The good things about the job.
- Why the job is right for you.
- Your answers to people who don't like it.
- What you can do to prepare for it.

Tell your group, or the class about your job.
Answer their questions.

BUSINESS STUDIES *in English*

There are about 11 million meetings in the USA every day. A meeting can be the best way to develop plans, motivate people and get action on good ideas. Yet studies show that over 50% of meeting time is wasted. Here are some ideas for better meetings.

Sales manager · Marketing consultant · Web designer · Accountant · Advertising agency account executive · Chairperson (Managing director)

1. **The right arrangement of seats for a meeting:**

 Creative brainstorm: everyone sits in a circle (more democratic).

 *Information/Training*: in a U-shape, so it's easier to see presentations.

 *Decision-making*: Chairperson sits in the middle, so he or she is in the best place to hear everyone else.

2. **If you're organising a meeting:**
   - Send everyone a note stating the meeting place, starting and finishing time.
   - Prepare an agenda – a list of the topics to discuss.
   - Use ICT and other tools like flip charts.
   - Name a person to take the minutes (write a report about the meeting).

3. **If you're attending a meeting:**
   - Read the agenda carefully.
   - Prepare information you need for the discussion.
   - Ask only important questions during the meeting. Don't go off track.

A Find words or phrases in the text which mean:
1 really makes people want to do something.
2 the person who leads the discussion.
3 a report on what was said in the meeting.
4 saying something that is not on the topic.

B With a partner, talk about these questions:
1 Are English language classes like business meetings?
2 Do you ever attend meetings? What are your feelings about them?

9 PORTFOLIO WRITING

Write a letter to a company to ask for more information about a job that has been advertised (70–100 words). Use the following expressions, but in the right order.
   a) Yours faithfully
   b) I'm interested in your advertisement for a job in .....
   c) I think this job is best for me because ....
   d) I'd like to know more about .... (salary, hours, place) ...
   e) Thank you for your help.
   f) Dear Sir or Madam

10 *Your answer:* WHAT KIND OF JOB IS BEST FOR YOU?

What do you think now? Is an interesting job more important than a high salary? Is it best to be your own boss? What is the most important thing for you in choosing a job? What is the best kind of job for you? An outdoor job? A challenging job?

SEE WORKBOOK UNIT 3

Last word:

Can you use all the language items below? Write *Yes*, *No*, or *Almost* against each.

Functions: Comparing

Language: Comparatives and superlatives

Vocabulary: Work; job satisfaction; meetings

Stranger than fiction

What's new?

Subject:	Entertainment
Functions:	Expressing likes and dislikes; talking about future plans and intentions
Language:	*going to* future

1 The BIG question:

ARE REALITY SHOWS GOOD TV?

FACT: The first reality TV show was *Survivor* in 2000. Today in the USA, reality shows make up about 20% of all TV programmes.

2 FOCUS ON ...

Words

A Match the TV shows with their definitions.

1	soap opera	a)	what happened in the world today.
2	talk show	b)	people answer questions or do activities to win prizes.
3	documentary	d)	a presenter asks people about their lives.
4	the news	e)	a daily or weekly story about the lives of fictional people.
5	game show	f)	a programme that gives information about an interesting topic.

1

B What sort of TV programmes do the photos show? Do you know any TV programmes like these?

C Put the words in the box in the correct sentences.

a) contestants   b) critic   c) producer   d) series   e) viewers

1 The most popular TV shows attract the most ....
2 The ..... of a programme is responsible for its organisation.
3 I can't wait for the new ...... of my favourite show.
4 A TV ...... writes reviews about programmes.
5 ...... try to win prizes on game shows.

2

D Combine the words from the text to make phrases.

1	look like	a)	plastic surgery
2	do	b)	spiders
3	eat	c)	gross
4	be	d)	a celebrity
5	have	e)	challenges

Ideas

A Use **Language Bank 6** to discuss with a partner what sorts of TV shows you like and don't like.

B Discuss these ideas with a partner:
1 Reality TV shows the real world.
2 Reality TV is harmless entertainment.

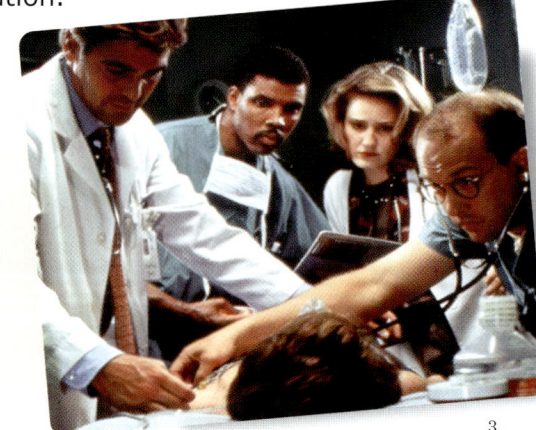
3

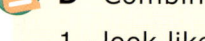

3   READING

A Look at the names of the TV shows and the photos. What do you think the two TV shows are about?

Tonight's TV: Is this reality?
by Robert Gilbert, TV CRITIC

I want a famous face (10.30pm)

Twins Mike and Matt had plastic surgery to look like Brad Pitt. And last week Jeanette had stomach and breast operations: "I'm going to be Kate Winslet," she said before the surgery. Tonight on *I Want a Famous Face* we're going to meet Jessica, who wants to be Jennifer Lopez. MTV's documentary series is about people who want to look like their favorite celebrity. It follows them before, during and after painful plastic surgery operations. The patients seem happy with their new faces and bodies, but they don't actually look like their favorite stars. Critics say the show trivializes plastic surgery and exploits people who feel bad about themselves. However, according to the MTV website, all the patients decided on their surgery and paid for it themselves; MTV just shows the operations. And having celebrity surgery seems to be a popular trend – there's going to be another series soon.

Lots of people want to look like stars such as Kate Winslet

Survivor (7pm)

Tonight's *Survivor* program is the last in the series. On tonight's show, the final three contestants are going to do their last challenges – including walking over hot coals. All three are going to try and win the million dollar prize.

Survivor is the old man of reality TV game shows. We know the story: 16 contestants on a tropical island who find food, make their own house, do challenges – and vote each other off the island. Viewers who *A contestant walks over hot coals* love watching the gross challenges of new reality game shows, find *Survivor* old-fashioned. Contestants don't lie in a box with rats or eat spiders and fish eyes. On *Survivor*, the contestants' challenges are hard, but the hardest and most important part is living together. This is why the show is special – and why it's such good TV. I'm certainly going to watch this one.

B 1 What sort of TV shows are described?
2 Were your ideas in A correct?
3 Summarise what happens on each show.

C Read these sentences about the two shows. Which are true (**T**) and which are false (**F**)? Why?

	T/F
1 On *I Want a Famous Face* people have plastic surgery on their face and body.	☐
2 Critics like *I Want a Famous Face*.	☐
3 After plastic surgery MTV patients look like their favourite stars.	☐
4 MTV is not going to make any more *Famous Face* programmes.	☐
5 *Survivor* is a documentary.	☐
6 Tonight a new series of *Survivor* starts.	☐
7 *Survivor* is a new show.	☐
8 The challenges on *Survivor* are gross.	☐

D 1 Do you think these programmes show reality?
2 Would you like to be on one of these shows? Which one? Why?/Why not?

4   LANGUAGE

A 1 Find six sentences in the article with ***going to***. Highlight them.
2 Do the sentences refer to past, present or future activities?
3 Are the actions in the sentences plans and intentions, or predictions?
4 How do we form the ***going to*** structure?

WORKBOOK UNIT 4: *GOING TO* FUTURE

Stranger than fiction

5 LISTEN IN

Trista Rehn and Ryan Sulter found true love on a reality TV show

Aimee Baum, a 32-year-old housewife from Las Vegas, after her appearance on a make-over TV show

A Before you listen, look at the photos of two TV programmes. Would you like to watch these shows?

B You are going to listen to three people talking about TV shows. First check the meaning of these words and phrases:

unattractive	beauty queen	dumb
worms	humiliate	they suck!

C Listen to the conversation and tick ✓ the correct boxes.

	Likes reality TV	Dislikes reality TV
Speaker 1		
Speaker 2		
Speaker 3		

D Listen again and write the correct speaker (**1**, **2** or **3**) for each statement.

1/2/3

a) I like reality shows. Some are really dumb. ☐

b) I'd love to be on a show like that and be famous. ☐

c) These shows just exploit and humiliate people. ☐

d) I love all the reality shows. ☐

e) It's not as real as you think. ☐

f) It's their own fault if they can't cope with problems. ☐

g) These people go on game shows for the money. ☐

Casting call: *Beautiful People*

We are looking for contestants for the next series of *Beautiful People*. We are looking for you and a friend, a cousin, a sister, mom, daughter, aunt or neighbor, to get a new face and body. Apply now!

6 YOUR TURN TO SPEAK

A Role play
Look at the internet casting call for *Beautiful People*. You would like to be on the show with your best friend but your friend doesn't want to do it. Can you persuade him *or* her?

B Conversation
Work with a partner. Use **Language Bank 7** to talk about the following:
1 What shows are you going to watch on TV this week? Why?
2 What programme are you definitely not going to watch?
3 What else are you going to do in your free time this week?

7 YOUR TOPIC

Choose a popular soap opera or game show on TV in your country. Make notes about:
● What sort of programme it is; how often it is on TV.
● Who the characters, presenters or contestants are.
● What happens in the show.
● Why you like or don't like it.

Tell your class about the programme. Answer their questions.

8 MEDIA STUDIES *in English*

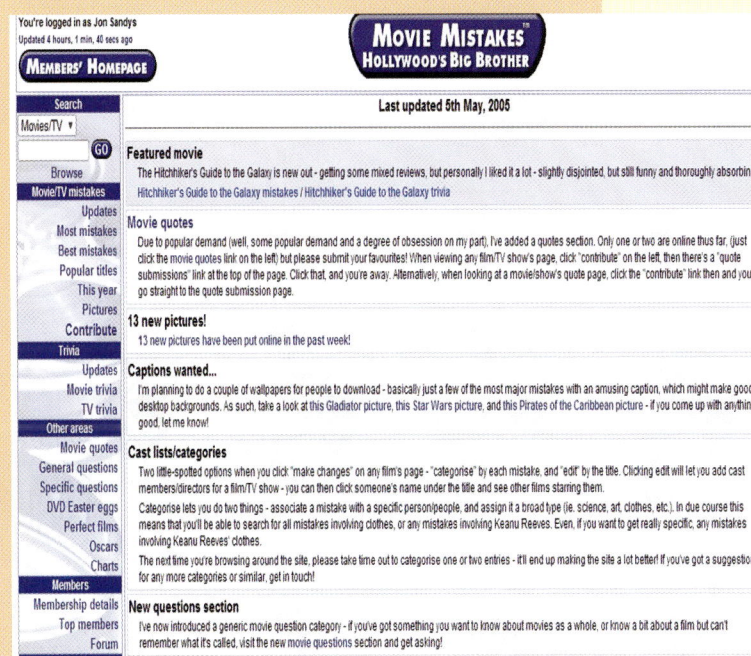

www.moviemistakes.com *shows continuity errors in thousands of films*

Continuity

In movies, continuity is making sure that the people, things, places and events stay the same in different shots or scenes. There are two types of continuity errors:

- **Visual errors:** things change colour and things change place or disappear in the same scene. Visual mistakes happen because the order of the filming is not the same as the order of the final movie. The crew perhaps films a scene from the end of a movie first, then one from the middle, and so on. Location, weather, the light, and the cast can all influence a shooting schedule.   5

                                                  10

- **Plot errors:** a mistake in the story of the movie. For example, a character says he was an only child, but later says he has a sister. Plot errors often happen in complicated science fiction or fantasy movies.   15

A Find words in the text which mean:
1 the story of a film (UK) / movie (US).
2 the team that make the film.
3 a part of the film.
4 a place outside the studio where filming takes place.
5 the actors in a film.
6 the timetable for filming a film.

B Say whether these mistakes are visual or plot errors.
1 *Terminator 3*: a plane's number changes from N3035C on the ground to N9373F in the air.
2 *Spider-Man*: Spider-Man throws two men into two windows and breaks them. A minute later the two windows are OK.
3 *Harry Potter and the Prisoner of Azkaban*: Arthur Weasley says to Harry, "Thirteen years ago, when you stopped you-know-who..." Harry is 13 now and was one year old when he stopped Voldemort. So Harry stopped Voldemort 12 years ago, not 13.

C 1 What is your favourite film? Why?
2 Can you remember any mistakes in films?

9 PORTFOLIO WRITING

Write a review of a film (120–150 words). Use the present tense for your review. Write three paragraphs. First, give the name of the film, what sort of film it is and who the actors are. Next describe what happens in it. Finally, say why you liked or disliked the film.

10 *Your answer:* ARE REALITY SHOWS GOOD TV?

Is reality TV real? Does it entertain people? Does it exploit contestants? Are TV shows and movies getting dumber?

SEE WORKBOOK UNIT 4

Last word:

Can you use all the language items below? Write *Yes*, *No*, or *Almost* against each.

Functions: Expressing likes and dislikes; talking about future plans and intentions

Language: *going to* future

Vocabulary: Television; films

What's new?

Subject:	Shops and shopping
Functions:	Complaining; quantifying
Language:	Adverbials of quantity

1 *The BIG question:* DO SHOPS RIP YOU OFF?

FACT: Most complaints from shoppers are about faulty goods, or problems connected with the shops' sales methods.

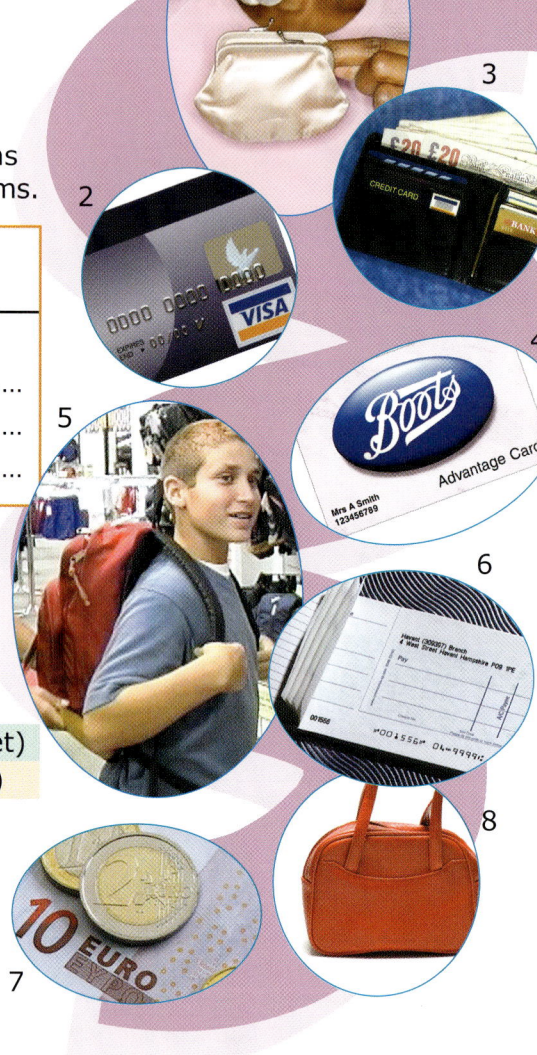

2 FOCUS ON ...

Words

A 1 What can you buy in these shops? Add three more items to each list. Then make lists with different shops and items.

Department store	Electronics shop	Newsagent	Sports shop
clothes	*cameras*	*magazines*	*footballs*
....	....	....	....
....	....	....	....
....	....	....	....

2 Work with a partner. Ask and answer the questions.
  a) What are your favourite shops? Why?
  b) Do you buy things you don't need? Why?

B 1 Match the photos with the words in the box.

a) cash   b) cheque (US: check)   c) purse (US: wallet)
d) backpack   e) credit card   f) handbag (US: purse)
g) wallet (US: billfold)   h) store card

2 Which are ways to pay? Which are places to keep money? Make two lists.
3 How do you usually pay for things?

C Choose the correct words for these definitions:

1	A **customer** is a person who ..... things.	a) *buys*	b) *sells*
2	A **sales assistant** is a person who ..... things.	a) *sells*	b) *repairs*
3	A **sale** is when prices are ..... than usual.	a) *higher*	b) *lower*
4	A **receipt** is a ..... that shows you paid for something.	a) *credit card*	b) *piece of paper*
5	A **refund** is when you get your ..... back.	a) *money*	b) *goods*

Ideas

Discuss these statements with a partner:
A It's easy to say 'no' to pushy sales assistants.
B Customer service isn't the most important thing about a shop.

3 READING

A Read these three letters. Which letter isn't from an unhappy customer?

Image magazine

READERS' CORNER

Here are some of your letters about shopping experiences and pushy sales assistants.

Dear Image

I was really down, so I went shopping, which always makes me feel better! The sales assistant persuaded me to have a store card. I didn't want one at all, but to shut her up I said 'yes'. Later, I felt 5 angry that she pressurised me into getting the card. Of course, I used it and spent more money than I can afford. So I'm paying every month. But I'm 10 still only paying back the interest! The interest on these cards is very 15 high but the sales assistants don't tell you about this. Store cards are 20 a real rip-off!
Rebecca

Dear Image

Last week I saw this crazy cell phone, which makes a noise that repels mosquitoes – perfect in summer! The sales assistant said it was a bargain. I 25 told him it was too expensive. Then he told me it was on a sale and offered me a discount. Stupidly, I said OK. At the cash desk I suddenly thought, "What am I doing? I don't need it," and said I 30 didn't want to buy it. The sales assistant was really rude to me, but I just left the store. It was a horrible experience but I'm glad I said 'no'.
Anna

Dear Image

Before you complain about service in 35 shops, think about the sales assistants a little! It's easy to criticise them, but there's a lot of pressure on them, too. I worked in a clothes shop. They trained us to approach customers 40 and persuade them to buy things. Some customers chose clothes that didn't suit them at all, but we always told them how great they looked. I didn't like that much. We also had 45 targets for getting customers to have store cards. And they made it really difficult for customers to get refunds. After six months I left because I hated working there.   *Laurence* 50

B Who did what? Rebecca [**R**], Anna [**A**], Laurence [**L**], or none of them [**N**]?
1 worked in a clothes shop
2 opened a store card account
3 didn't like the sales methods at his workplace
4 doesn't want a new mobile phone
5 asked for a receipt when buying something
6 is paying lots of interest
7 met a rude sales assistant
8 told customers they looked great
9 walked out of the shop without buying anything
10 asked for a refund

C What do you think?
1 Were Rebecca and Anna silly?
2 Do you agree with Laurence's point of view?

D Tell the class about your best and worst shopping experiences.

4 LANGUAGE

A Look at the adverbials of quantity in **bold**. Give each one the correct symbol.

++	+	–	––

1 The clothes didn't suit them ***at all***.
2 I enjoy shopping ***a lot***. / I liked it ***very much***.
3 I did**n't** like that ***much***.
4 Think about the sales assistants ***a little***.

WORKBOOK UNIT 5: ADVERBIALS OF QUANTITY

5 LISTEN IN

A You are going to listen to a customer complaining on the telephone. Do you like complaining? Do you find it difficult?

B Listen to the conversation. Why didn't Lucy get the correct order?

C Listen again and complete these sentences:
1 Lucy speaks to Debbie from .... Services.
2 Lucy ordered some goods from a ....
3 Instead of a .... by Robbie Williams, she got one by Coldplay.
4 Instead of a black backpack, Lucy got a ....
5 She wanted the backpack for her brother's ....
6 Lucy wants to speak to the ......
7 The free gift is .... It's got a hole in it.
8 Lucy can .... the wrong goods.

D Answer these questions:
1 How did Lucy feel when she spoke to Debbie? Why did she shout?
2 How do people you know complain? Are they polite? Do they shout? What about you?

6 YOUR TURN TO SPEAK

A Role play
Work with a partner. Use **Language Bank 8.**
Customer in a shop: You bought a camera last weekend, but it doesn't work. Take it back and complain. Ask for a refund.
Shop assistant: You can't give a refund. Offer an exchange, or a credit note.

B Conversation
Work with a partner. Use **Language Bank 9** to talk about how much and why you like:
1 shopping for clothes
2 shopping for food
3 shopping in sales
4 large shopping centres
5 sales assistants

7 YOUR TOPIC

Think about your best or worst buy.
Make notes about:
● What sort of item it is
● When and where you bought it
● How much you paid for it
● Why it was a good or bad buy
Tell your class about your item. Answer their questions.

8 **CONSUMER RIGHTS** *in English*

TIPS FOR ONLINE SHOPPERS

Within five years, a quarter of all UK shopping will be online. But is it safe? Here are some useful tips to avoid rip-offs:

Before you buy:
- Use companies that you or a lot of your friends know.
- Check that the company has a full postal address and telephone number.
- Check that the website has a secure way of paying (look for the padlock symbol 🔒).
- Does the company have a privacy statement? Check what they do with your personal information.

Know your rights:
- Your consumer rights online are the same as when you buy from a shop.
- The company must send you confirmation of your order.
- You have the right to cancel an order within a certain time.

When you buy:
- Don't give personal information that isn't necessary to buy something.
- Don't send your credit card number in an email – emails aren't secure.
- Check that your credit card statement is correct.
- Print out a copy of the website information, your order and any emails to the company.

A Find words or phrases in the text which mean:
1. where the company's office is.
2. safe, so your money goes to the right place.
3. an explanation about use of personal information.
4. laws that protect shoppers.
5. written proof that you have bought something.
6. a request to buy something.
7. to stop your online order.
8. the list of what you have spent on your credit card.

B With a partner, discuss:
1. Which is the most useful tip? Why?
2. What products or services are best to buy online?

C Do you use the internet to shop?
1. If 'yes': What do you buy? Who from? Do you have any tips?
2. If 'no': Why not?

9 PORTFOLIO WRITING

You have bought a product online. Write an email to the company and complain that there is something wrong with it. Write about what you bought and when, what the problem is and what you want the company to do (70–80 words).

10 *Your answer:* DO SHOPS RIP YOU OFF?

Are you a shopaholic? Are sales assistants pushy? Do you know your rights?

 SEE WORKBOOK UNIT 5

Last word:

Can you use all the language items below? Write *Yes*, *No*, or *Almost* against each.

Functions:	Complaining; quantifying
Language:	Adverbials of quantity
Vocabulary:	Shops; shopping

Eat your greens!

What's new?

Topic:	Food
Functions:	Giving reasons; making and replying to requests
Language:	Connecting words: *and*, *but* and *because*

1 *The BIG question:*

MUST WE KILL TO EAT?

FACT: There are over 3 million vegetarians in the UK. That's 5% of the adult population.

2 FOCUS ON ...

Words

A Add as many words to each food group as you can.

1 Vegetables: *lettuce* ...

2 Dairy produce: *milk* ...

3 Meat: *lamb* ...

4 Fish: *salmon* ...

5 Fruit: *oranges* ...

B The words in the box can describe food. Which are positive ➕ which are negative ➖ ?

bland	delicious	disgusting	fantastic	healthy	horrible	tasty	mouthwatering

C Work with a partner. Ask and answer the questions:
1. What are your favourite foods?
2. What foods don't you eat?
3. What foods or dishes are popular in your region, or country?
4. Are you, or any of your friends or family, a vegetarian?

D These words are in the text on the page opposite. Match them with the correct definitions:

1. livestock
2. global warming
3. methane
4. nutrients
5. soil
6. heart disease
7. research
8. leather

a) plants grow in this
b) animals kept for food
c) scientific study of something
d) the increase in temperature of the world's atmosphere
e) a gas that contributes to global warming
f) illness that stops the heart working properly
g) animal skin used for shoes and bags
h) these make plants, animals or people grow

Ideas

Discuss these statements with a partner:
A Vegetarians are unhealthy because they don't eat meat.
B People become vegetarians because they don't like the taste of meat.

3   READING

A   Read the article quickly. Is it for or against vegetarianism?

6

VEGETARIANISM – THE FACTS

Vegetarians eat no meat or fish. Most vegetarians eat dairy produce and eggs. Vegans don't eat any animal products, including dairy produce, eggs and honey, and they don't wear leather shoes. You can buy mouth-watering vegetarian food almost everywhere and it is cheaper than meat or fish. But most people become vegetarians because it is better for 5 animals, for the environment and their own health.

Better for animals

About 10 billion animals die to produce meat each year in the USA. That's about 35 animals per person! These animals live short, miserable lives in terrible conditions. Their food is full of chemicals. Some animals have to 10 travel to markets without enough food, water and air.

Better for the environment

When large numbers of animals live on small areas of land, they take away the nutrients from the soil and kill plants. Livestock also produce about 25% of methane gas in the UK and this contributes to global 15 warming. A cow produces one kilo of methane for every two kilos of meat! Producing meat is a waste of good land, too. Half a hectare of land can produce about 4,500 kg of beans, 13,650 kg of carrots, 22,730 kg of tomatoes but only 114 kg of beef. It takes 900 litres of water to produce one kilo of wheat but it takes 100,000 litres to produce one kilo of meat. 20 People in poor countries are hungry and thirsty but we waste water and food on livestock. And in countries such as Brazil, farmers cut down huge areas of rainforest to create land for livestock.

Better for health

Vegetarian food is a healthy choice. Research shows that a vegetarian diet 25 can reduce illness and disease. And after problems such as BSE (mad cow disease), isn't it better not to eat meat at all?

Sheep crowded into a truck

Rainforest is cut down for cattle

B   Answer these questions:
1   What is the difference between a vegetarian and a vegan?
2   How many animals die each year to provide food in the USA?
3   How do livestock contribute to global warming?
4   How can we best use land and water to produce food?

C   Find these figures in the text. What do they refer to?

35	25%	114	100,000

D   Where do you think this text comes from? Who wrote it? What was the writer's intention in writing it? What effect does he or she want to have on the reader?

4   LANGUAGE

Look at the connecting words (***and, but*** and ***because***) in these sentences.
* You can buy vegetarian food everywhere **and** it is cheaper than meat.
* Most people become vegetarians **because** it is better for animals.
* People in poor countries are hungry **but** we waste food on livestock.

A   Which connecting word adds a reason?
B   Which connecting word adds another positive or similar idea?
C   Which connecting word adds a contrasting idea?

WORKBOOK UNIT 6:
CONNECTING WORDS
AND, BUT AND *BECAUSE*

5 **LISTEN IN**

A Before you listen, look at the picture. What does it show?

1 Do you go to restaurants with food like this? What is good ➕ and bad ➖ about them?

2 How often do you eat out? What is your favourite restaurant or café?

B You are going to listen to a conversation between Ellen and her boyfriend Dan, who are going out to eat. First check the meaning of these words:

| iron | GM (genetically modified) food | vitamins |
| cruel | care about | genes |

C Listen to the conversation.
Why is Dan angry with Ellen?

Combination Meals	
1/2 lb. Burger, Fries and Dessert	$9.95
Grilled Chicken Sandwich, Fries and Dessert	$8.95
1/2 lb. Triple Cheeseburger, Fries and Dessert	$10.95
Big Bowl Salads	
Caesar Salad	$7.95
Steak Salad	$9.95
Vegetarian Salad	$4.95

D Read these sentences. Then listen again and tick ✅ the arguments Dan mentions.

1 Vegetarians are unhealthy. ☐
2 Vegetarians are boring. ☐
3 Vegetarian food tastes good. ☐
4 Animals aren't as important as humans. ☐
5 It's cruel to kill plants. ☐
6 GM foods are necessary to reduce world hunger. ☐
7 GM foods are healthy. ☐
8 Where food comes from is important. ☐
9 People have to be free to choose. ☐
10 Meat tastes best. ☐

E Can you think of other arguments for eating meat, or not eating meat?

F Is Dan still Ellen's boyfriend? What do you think?

6 YOUR TURN TO SPEAK

A Conversation

Use the **Language Bank 10** to discuss these questions with your partner. Give reasons for each answer.

1 Is it cruel to kill plants?
2 Why does producing meat contribute to world hunger?
3 Are GM foods dangerous?

B Role play

Use the menu on this page and **Language Bank 11** to order food in a hamburger restaurant. In pairs, play the roles of the customer and the sales assistant.

7 YOUR TOPIC

Work with a partner. One partner presents the advantages of vegetarianism to the Director of The American Meat Industry Association. The other presents the advantages of eating meat to the Vegan Diet Association's Health Director. Make notes about:

• Vegetarianism and health
• The lives of animals
• Meat and the environment
• Food I like to eat

The Director asks questions.

8 NUTRITION in English

The Food Guide Pyramid is a US government guide to a healthy diet. It shows the right number of servings of different foods per
5 day. You must eat different foods to get the right nutrients and the right number of calories for your weight. The fats, oils and sweets group is in the smallest part at
10 the top of the pyramid because most people eat too many sweets and too much fat, especially saturated fat. The most important foods from the five
15 major food groups are in the three lower parts of the pyramid. Each of these food groups provides some, but not all, of the nutrients you need. Foods in one
20 group can't replace foods in another group. For good health, you need them all.

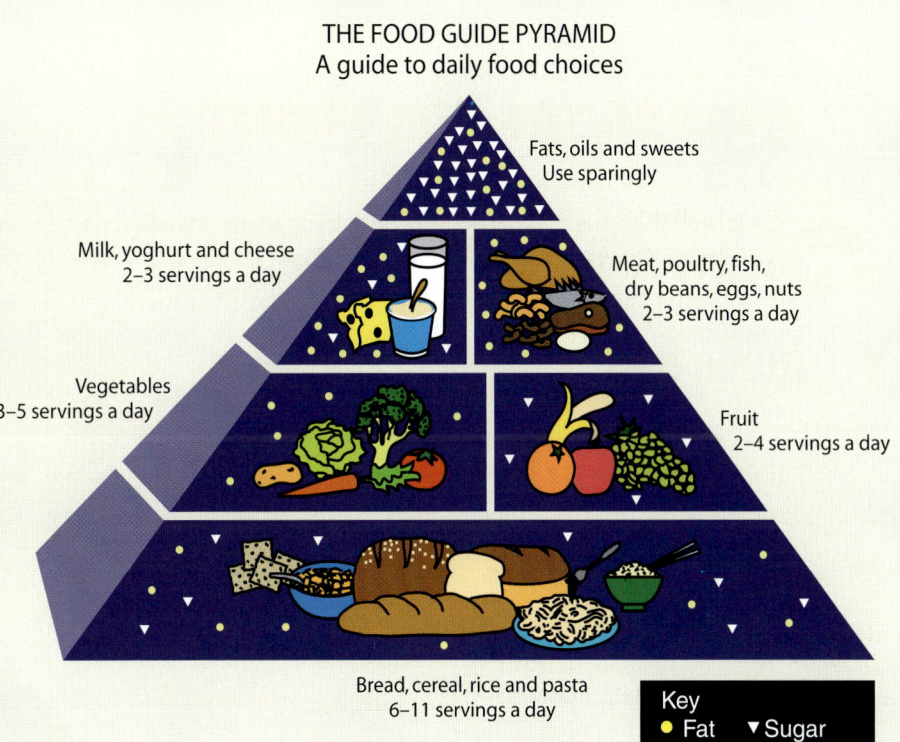

THE FOOD GUIDE PYRAMID
A guide to daily food choices

Fats, oils and sweets
Use sparingly

Milk, yoghurt and cheese
2–3 servings a day

Meat, poultry, fish, dry beans, eggs, nuts
2–3 servings a day

Vegetables
3–5 servings a day

Fruit
2–4 servings a day

Bread, cereal, rice and pasta
6–11 servings a day

Key
● Fat   ▼ Sugar

A Find words and phrases in the diagram and the text which mean:
1 in small amounts, or not very often
2 an amount of food
3 everything that you eat
4 measurements of the energy in food
5 how heavy you are
6 unhealthy fat
7 categories of foods with the same nutrients
8 the condition of your body

B Read the text again and answer these questions:
1 Why is the *Fats, oils and sweets* group at the top of the pyramid?
2 Why is the *Bread and pasta* group at the bottom?
3 Why do we need to eat foods from all food groups?

C According to the pyramid, is a vegetarian diet a healthy diet?

9 PORTFOLIO WRITING

Write a report for a health magazine (120–150 words). Explain what is a healthy diet. Compare a vegetarian diet and a meat diet.

10 *Your answer:* MUST WE KILL TO EAT?

Must we kill animals for food? Is vegetarian food tasty? Are vegetarians healthier than meat-eaters?

SEE WORKBOOK UNIT 6

Last word:

Can you use all the language items below? Write *Yes*, *No*, or *Almost* against each.

Functions: Giving reasons; making and replying to requests

Language: Connecting words: *and*, *but* and *because*

Vocabulary: Food; nutrition

For your eyes only

What's new?

Subject:	Diaries, blogs
Functions:	Talking about events in the indefinite and recent past
Language:	Present perfect with *ever*, *never*, *just*

1 ___The BIG question:___

WHAT DO YOU KEEP PRIVATE?

FACT: In 1999 there were only 23 blogs on the internet. Now there are over 70 million blogs on the internet with 120,000 new ones every day.

2 FOCUS ON …

Words

A Put the feelings in the correct lists.

happy	sad	depressed	angry	excited
upset	proud	lonely	scared	relieved

Good feelings	Bad feelings
happy	……
……	……

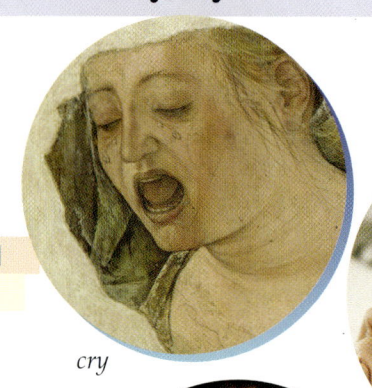

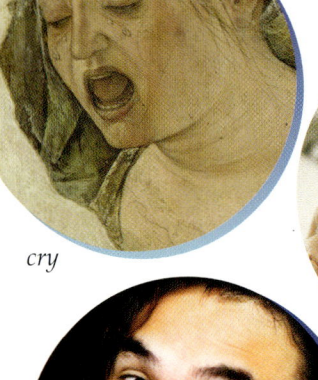

cry

chat

B 1 Add more words and phrases using the pictures.

Things I do in private	Things I do in public
• Cry if I'm sad	• Chat with my best friend
• ……	• ……

2 Work with a partner. Compare your lists.
a) Do you do the same things in private? And in public?
b) Do you show your feelings in public?

clean your teeth

C Match these words and their definitions.

1	self-exposure	a) dealing with your problems by yourself
2	self-control	b) feeling sure about what you can do
3	self-confidence	c) showing your private feelings to the world
4	self-help	d) remaining calm even if you're angry or upset

D Complete the sentences with the correct words.

1 If you write your diary as a website, you're a …   a) access.
2 When you put details on a website, you are …   b) editor.
3 If you can use the internet, you've got …   c) blogger.
4 A person who reads and corrects your work is an …   d) editor.
     e) posting them.

dance

Ideas

Discuss these statements with a partner:
A The internet is the best way of communicating we've ever had.
B Private things are private – don't make them public.

3 READING

A Read the website quickly. How are blogs different to diaries in the past?

Writing a blog   *Writing a diary*

What bloggers say

Blogs are a great way to find friends on the internet with the same interests as you.
Ben

More...

LINKS
Audio blogs

Photo blogs

Other blogs

Fashion (253)

Cars (356)

Travel (1743)

Have you ever wanted to tell people about your secret loves and hates? Have you ever shouted in public when you were angry or upset? Have you ever done something awful, then felt better after you told a friend? A blog gives you the chance to do just that … and more! Blogs are online diaries where writers post details about their lives and thoughts for anyone to read. In the past, diaries were usually private. Some people published their diaries – but a long time after the events in them. Blogs are different: your diary and photos can be on the web in seconds! You can also get immediate feedback from your readers. 5

Here are just a few reasons to write a blog:
- You can publish news as it happens – and you don't need to be a professional journalist. Salam Pax, the famous Baghdad blogger, wrote about daily life during the Iraq War in 2003. "This is better than anything in the newspapers," said one reader. "We really feel what it is like when bombs fall around you." 10
- You can practise your writing skills. "I have complete freedom to publish my work online – without an editor changing things," says Tom Grant. "Writers have never had such a wonderful chance."
- You can share your feelings. "When my mother died, I was really depressed," says 16-year-old Kelly. "I had nobody to talk to, so last month I started a blog. I've had so much help from complete strangers."
- You can communicate personal experiences. "My boyfriend Sam and I write about everything in our blogs," 15 says Emma Brown. "Sam has just proposed to me online in his blog – so romantic! How did I say 'yes'? In my blog, of course!"

← BACK   CREATE A BLOG NOW   FAQs   CONTACT   CONTINUE →

B Answer the questions. Who …
1 used the internet to communicate an important decision?
2 got help with a personal experience?
3 wrote exactly what he wanted to write?
4 told people about life during a war?

C Discuss these questions with your class:
1 Read the three questions at the beginning of the website again. Is it easier to do these things online?
2 Do you think proposing online is romantic?
3 Have you ever blogged? When? What did you write about?

4 LANGUAGE

A Read the sentences and answer the questions.
- **Have** you ever **shouted** in public?
- Salam Pax **wrote** about life during the Iraq War in 2003.
- Sam **has** just **proposed** to me online.
- Last month I **started** a blog.

Which sentences refer to …
1 actions at a definite time in the past?
2 actions at an indefinite time in the past?

WORKBOOK UNIT 7: THE PRESENT PERFECT
WITH *EVER, NEVER, JUST*

For your eyes only

 5 **LISTEN IN**

A Before you listen, look at the pictures. How would you describe the feelings of the people in the pictures?

B You are going to listen to a conversation between Lizzie and Josh. First check the meanings of these words.

• self-centred	• rubbish
• nerd	• properly

C Listen to the conversation. Are these sentences true (**T**) or false (**F**)?   **T/F**

1 Lizzie is happy that Josh wrote about her on his website. ☐
2 Josh has written terrible things about Lizzie. ☐
3 Men write most web diaries. ☐
4 Lizzie thinks most blogs aren't very interesting. ☐
5 Lizzie thinks we spend too much time on the internet. ☐

D Add Lizzie's reasons against writing a web diary.

For writing a web diary	Against writing a web diary
• You can tell other people your feelings.	•
• You can write about anything you want.	•
• It's a good way to meet new people.	•

E What do you think?
1 Is Josh a loving person or a self-centred computer nerd?
2 Would you like to keep a web diary? Why / why not?

6 YOUR TURN TO SPEAK

A Role play
Your friend wants to set up a website for the class to compare ideas about their teachers. Persuade him / her that this is not going to help relationships between teachers and students.

B Conversation
Work with a partner. Use **Language Bank 12** to talk about if you have ever:
1 designed or set up a website
2 used a chat room
3 made a friend on the internet
4 written emails in English

7 YOUR TOPIC

Think about recent experiences you have had. Make notes about:
• something that has happened at school or in a public place
• something that has happened at home
• a happy experience
• an experience that made you feel sad, angry or scared
Make a presentation to your class about your experiences. Answer their questions.

8 CREATIVE WRITING in English

Want to improve your writing skills? Want to write interesting pieces that people can't wait to read? Here are some writing tips.

1 GETTING STARTED
- Brainstorm ideas: write down as many ideas as you can, as quickly as you can.
- Think about your readers and write for them.
- Make an outline of what you want to say. Use bullet points.

2 WHILE WRITING
- Have you got a beginning, a middle and an end?
- Is your first sentence an attention-getter?
- Does the main story make sense?
- Are any words or sentences unnecessary?
- Is the end interesting?
- Can you spot any mistakes?

3 REVISING AND PUBLISHING
- Read your work aloud. Is it clear?
- Check your grammar, spelling and punctuation.
- Read everything again.
- Ask someone else to check it.

"The Writer" by Giancarlo Neri

A creative writing group

A Find words or phrases in the text that mean:
1 make something better
2 think of lots of ideas in a short time
3 a mark like this: ●
4 plan
5 really interesting
6 find things that are wrong

B Answer the questions.
1 What do you find most difficult when you write in English?
  a) making it clear
  b) making it interesting
  c) spotting mistakes
  d) other difficulties (say what they are)
2 Which tips do you usually follow when you write?
3 Is there a tip you would like to try?

C Look at the pictures. What do you think: Is creative writing something you do alone or in a group?

9 PORTFOLIO WRITING

Write a website diary about something that has happened to you recently. Explain what happened, how you felt, and how the story ended. Follow the tips above (120–150 words).

10 *Your answer:* WHAT DO YOU KEEP PRIVATE?

Is self-exposure on blogs a good thing? Are there some things that are too private to talk about with strangers? Is the internet the best way to communicate?

SEE WORKBOOK UNIT 7

Last word:

Can you use all the language items below? Write *Yes*, *No*, or *Almost* against each.

Functions: Talking about events in the indefinite and recent past

Language: Present perfect with *ever*, *never* and *just*

Vocabulary: The internet; personal events; writing skills

Fashionistas

What's new?

Subject:	Fashion
Functions:	Talking on the phone; expressing preferences
Language:	Articles

1 *The BIG question:* ARE YOU A FASHION LEADER?

FACT: Japanese consumers buy a quarter of the world's luxury fashion goods.

2 FOCUS ON ...

Words

A 1 Make a list of as many clothing items as you can. Then compare your list with a partner.

2 Put the fashion accessories in the correct lists.

> bag bracelet earrings hat
> mobile phone music player necklace
> scarf sunglasses watch

Jewellery	Electronics	Other accessories

Tokyo: world capital of street fashion

B 1 Match the adjectives with the correct pictures.

a) spotted b) patterned c) plain d) striped e) checked

1	2	3	4	5

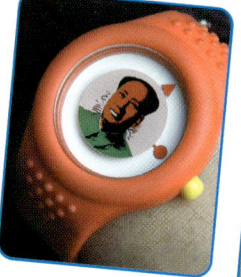

Accessories

 2 These adjectives (1–6) are in the text on page 37. Match each one with the correct definition.

1	baggy	a)	fashionable
2	flamboyant	b)	relaxed, not formal
3	smart	c)	tidy and well-dressed
4	cool	d)	eye-catching
5	comfortable	e)	big and loose
6	casual	f)	easy to wear

3 What are the people wearing in the pictures on these pages? Use the words in **A** and **B** to describe them. What do you think of the styles?

C Work with a partner. Ask and answer the questions.
1 What do you usually wear?
2 Do you spend a lot of money on clothes? How often do you go shopping for clothes?

Ideas
Discuss these questions:
A Do clothes and accessories express your personality?
B Is it important to follow fashion trends?
C What is street fashion?

3 READING

A Read the descriptions. Which three fashions do you like best?

a) Ms Fashion Slave follows the fashion magazines and copies what famous people wear. She is always looking for the latest 'in' look and spends a lot of money on fashion accessories.

b) Mr Brand wears expensive brands from head to toe: hat, underwear and socks. He likes to belong to a group. He always wants the latest running shoes. He feels more confident when wearing lots of logos.

c) Ms Individual is a creative fashion leader. She buys clothes in second-hand shops and makes her own street fashion. She mixes old with new, and patterned clothes with plain ones.

d) Ms Gothic wears black and white clothes, with white face make-up. Hair dyed in bright colours completes the look. Her friends all like the same style.

e) Mr Hip-hop wears very smart striped suits or baggy street fashion. He has an expensive haircut and a gold watch. He always wears cool designer sunglasses and lots of flamboyant jewellery to match the watch.

f) Ms Eco buys organic cotton dresses and cheap blouses in ethnic shops. She wears sandals, a spotted headscarf and wooden jewellery.

g) Mr Strong Man wears military, or comfortable country-style clothes: khaki trousers, big boots and casual checked shirts all through the year.

h) Miss Professional buys expensive designer suits. She wears skirts and shirts in plain, matching colours. She wants to show that she is successful and good at her job.

B 1 Which fashionistas wear these clothes?

  a) Individual styles ....
  b) Brands and logos ....
  c) Second-hand or cheap clothes ....
  d) Expensive clothes or accessories ....
  e) The same style as other people ....
  f) Casual clothes ....

C Which type of fashionista are you? If your type isn't here, write a new description.

D What do you think?
  1 Are fashion and style the same thing?
  2 Are famous people fashion role models?
  3 Is fashion only for the rich?

4 LANGUAGE

A Look at the sentences and answer the questions:
  a) She is always wearing **the** latest 'in' look.
  b) She copies what **famous people** wear.
  c) He likes to belong to **a** group.
  d) He wears **a** gold watch. His jewellery matches **the** watch.

B 1 Which sentence uses the indefinite article **a** to talk about:
      .... something for the first time?
      .... something in general
      (not a special or particular thing)?
  2 Which sentence uses the definite article **the** to talk about:
      .... something in particular?
      .... something again?
  3 Which sentence uses **no article** to talk about things in general?

WORKBOOK UNIT 8: ARTICLES

 5   LISTEN IN

A   Before you listen, look at the photos. What do you use your mobile phone for?

B   Listen to people talking about their mobile phones. Match the speakers to the reason they usually use their phone.

1 Martin	2 Lindy	3 Erica
4 Thomas	5 Mike	6 Roz

a) using email and calling customers ....

b) sending video messages and listening to music ....

c) chatting with friends ....

d) dating girls and watching football ....

e) playing games and sending texts ....

f) as a fashion accessory ....

C   Listen again and complete these sentences.
1   My girlfriend and I .... all the time.
2   I have different covers so it always .... my look.
3   Once I used a text to dump a ....
4   Sometimes I .... music and listen to it.
5   Please leave a .... after the beep.

D   Are mobile phones fashion accessories? Is it uncool not to have the latest phone? What about other electronic accessories?

6   YOUR TURN TO SPEAK

A   **Role play**
Work with a partner. Use **Language Bank 13** to role play a telephone conversation. You phone your friend about going shopping tomorrow but your friend is out. Leave a message with your friend's brother or sister. Suggest a time and place to meet.

B   **Conversation**
Work with a partner. Use **Language Bank 14** to talk about the sort of clothes and fashion accessories you prefer. Think about:

- style of clothes (Gothic, casual)
- kinds of accessories
- colours and patterns
- how well it fits (loose, tight)
- cost
- brands

7   YOUR TOPIC

Choose an item of clothing or a fashion accessory that you own. Make notes about:
- what it is
- what colour and what pattern
- where you bought it
- how expensive it was
- why you like or don't like it
- what it tells the world about you

Tell your class about your fashion item. Answer their questions.

8 GLOBALISATION in English

Where do your clothes come from? Globalisation means that we buy fashions from all over the world. That means cheaper clothes for people in richer countries and jobs for people in poorer countries such as Uzbekistan, or Nicaragua.

5

But globalisation also means that some big brand companies pay their suppliers very little. Women in factories in San Salvador make over a hundred pairs of trousers an hour, and earn only 75 pence for them. Growing cotton cheaply harms workers and the environment. Cotton farming uses chemicals that are dangerous to humans and animals and cause pollution. That's why many people today want sustainable clothing: clothes from companies that respect our world and workers' rights. In a survey, 98% of young people said that they don't buy products from companies that exploit workers and harm the environment.

10

15

20

25

Clothing factory in Nicaragua

Cotton farmer in Uzbekistan

YOU CAN:
- buy clothes made from organic cotton.
- buy from fair trade companies that pay farmers and workers properly.
- buy clothes from companies that make clothes locally.
- buy second-hand clothes.

A Find words or expressions that mean:
1. The companies who make clothes for big brands.
2. The places where workers make clothes.
3. Doesn't harm the environment or workers.
4. Not pay somebody enough for work.

B With a partner, talk about these questions:
1. What is good about globalisation?
2. What is bad about globalisation?
3. What effect does globalisation have on you?

C Which of the things in the **YOU CAN** list do you do? Why / why not?

9 PORTFOLIO WRITING

A You bought some organic cotton T-shirts from a fair trade clothing company yesterday. Write an email to tell a friend why they are better than normal T-shirts (70–80 words).

B Write a letter or an email to a friend describing the latest fashion (70–80 words).

10 *Your answer:* ARE YOU A FASHION LEADER?

Are you interested in fashion? What is your look? Do you like street fashion? Do you care where clothes come from? Do you wear second-hand clothes?

SEE WORKBOOK UNIT 8

Last word:

Can you use all the language items below? Write *Yes*, *No*, or *Almost* against each.

Functions: Talking on the phone; expressing preferences

Language: Articles

Vocabulary: Fashion; globalisation

1   The BIG read: AROUND THE WORLD IN 71 DAYS
Ellen MacArthur

Ellen MacArthur
1976: Born on July 8 in Derbyshire, England
1980: First went sailing with her aunt
1988: Bought her first boat
1995: Sailed solo around Britain
1997: Sailed solo across the Atlantic
2001: Second in the Vendée Globe (round the world) race
2005: Became the fastest person to sail solo around the world,
      in a time of 71 days, 14 hours, 18 minutes and 33 seconds

2   READING

A   Read the interview with Ellen MacArthur after her record solo voyage around the world.
1   Why did she do it?
2   Was she lonely on her voyage?

B   Read the interview again more carefully. Find these words and phrases in **bold** in the interview and choose the correct meaning.
1   bucket   a) something that holds water
   b) a luxury shower
   c) a machine that makes water warm
2   expanses   a) wide spaces
   b) sea animals   c) good weather
3   survival   a) having a good time
   b) staying alive
   c) thinking about the meaning of life
4   meteorologist   a) food expert
   b) computer expert   c) weather expert
5   soul   a) true love
   b) abilities and skills
   c) deepest thoughts and feelings
6   naps   a) short sleeps
   b) long sleeps   c) time awake

C   Choose the correct alternatives.
1   Ellen MacArthur is an *average / extraordinary* person.
2   Sailing alone is a *dangerous / relaxing* experience.
3   Daily life on the water is *very different from / quite similar to* life on land.

D   Answer the questions.
1   Why does Ellen sail?
2   What is dangerous out at sea? What is the most important thing?
3   What else is important in Ellen's life? What do you think of her answer?

E   What did Ellen say about the practical side of sailing alone? Make notes about these points.
1   What did she eat? Why?
2   How often did she sleep? When?
3   How did she wash? How often?

3   YOUR TURN TO SPEAK

Work with a partner or in a small group and discuss these questions:
A   1   What kind of person do you think Ellen MacArthur is? How would you describe her?
2   Ellen's boat cost €3 million and was full of the latest technology. Is this real sailing?

B   Imagine you are going to be alone at sea for three months. Decide:
1   which three important things you would like to take with you
2   what you would miss most
3   which person you would like to see first when you come back

C   Did you enjoy reading this interview? Why? / Why not?

9

Never sleeping for more than an hour at a time, living off freeze-dried food and washing in a **bucket** *is not everyone's idea of a good time. But* **Ellen MacArthur**, *who has just broken the record for sailing solo round the world, is not your average person, as the SPIEGEL ONLINE interviewer discovered.*

Interviewer: You've just sailed around the world faster than anyone has ever done before. You knew that if you met an iceberg or a big ship during the night you'd probably be dead. Have you ever asked yourself why you did it?

MacArthur: No, never. I knew it wasn't a holiday trip – and I knew why I was out there.

Interviewer: Why was that exactly?

MacArthur: I love sailing. I loved it even as a little girl. I enjoy the **expanses** of the oceans. I'm happy with that and I've never wanted anything else.

Interviewer: Pete Goss said, "I don't sail out there to become a different person, find my **soul** or any of that stuff. I just want to sail." Does that apply to you too?

MacArthur: I couldn't put it better myself.

Interviewer: How does your life on the water differ from your life on land?

MacArthur: It's different in every respect. On the water there's no 24-hour rhythm and no day is like any other. Everything is about **survival**: you sleep when the weather lets you, you eat because you have to. Eating on board is never a pleasure. I just mix freeze-dried food with hot water. On board I don't need to be a cook.

Interviewer: But apart from that you're a navigator, **meteorologist** …'

MacArthur: … mechanic, computer expert, doctor. I have to treat my injuries myself, repair hard discs and webcams and the sails …

Interviewer: Is there any difference between night and day?

MacArthur: Only in what you can see.

Interviewer: How do you organise your sleep?

MacArthur: In as many **naps** as possible, most of them 20 minutes or less. I rarely sleep for a whole hour. There's no plan for sleep. You have to take every chance you get.

Interviewer: You didn't have a shower on board for your voyage. Did that bother you?

MacArthur: It doesn't matter, because there's no-one on board to tell you that you smell. Once I washed myself with a bucket of water, another time I showered in the rain. It's very important to make sure the webcam's switched off though!

Interviewer: People followed your voyage over the internet, you kept a diary and gave interviews, you had e-mails sent by fans and you filmed yourself. Did you want to give deep-sea sports a face?

MacArthur: No. The idea was a different one: although I was alone at sea, modern communications meant that I was never lonely. I tried to share my experiences with others.

Interviewer: Is there any room in your life for other things apart from sailing: a boyfriend, a family of your own?

MacArthur: No, not really.

Interviewer: Ms. MacArthur, thank you for the interview.

Adapted and reproduced by permission of SPIEGEL. net GmbH

Rule of law

1 *The BIG question:*

WHO NEEDS RULES?

FACT: In a survey, two-thirds of British people said there are too many laws and restrictions.

2 FOCUS ON ...

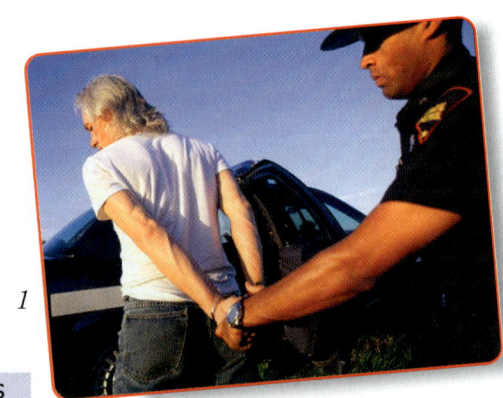

1

Words

| drinking alcohol | dropping litter | fraud | using mobile phones |
| taking photos | murder | shoplifting | smoking | talking | graffiti |

A  1 Which of these things in the word box are:
a) always illegal (against the law)?
b) sometimes not allowed, or against the rules in certain places?
Complete the table, then add one more thing to each list.

Always illegal	Sometimes not allowed
• fraud	• drinking alcohol
•	• ....

2 Look at the second list again. Where and when are these things not allowed? Why?

B With a partner, ask and answer these questions.
1 What rules are there at your school or workplace?
2 Do you think all these rules are necessary?

C 1 Match the correct phrases to the pictures.
a) committing a crime
b) arresting a criminal
c) being in prison

2

3

D  Look at these words from the text. Cross out one verb that is incorrect for each group.

make		give up		collect		live in a	
do	rules	share	possessions	want	freedom	join a	commune
break		develop		defend		risk a	
obey		have		like		leave a	

Ideas

Discuss these statements with a partner:
A Everybody breaks rules.
B People who break laws should go to prison.

3   READING

A   Look at the photo. What do you think is happening?

B   Read the article quickly. Choose the best title.

| 1   Happy memories | 2   A Life in Orange | 3   Ninety-three Rolls Royces |

When Tim Guest was four years old, his mother became a follower of the Indian guru, Bhagwan Shree Rajneesh. She dyed all[5] her clothes orange – all Bhagwan's followers had to wear the colours of the sun. But while followers of other gurus[10] have to give up a lot of things, Bhagwan's followers didn't have to obey many other rules. The guru's philosophy[15] was "the more you risk, the more you grow". There was lots of singing, dancing and meditating. Bhagwhan himself liked[20] collecting Rolls Royces (he had 93) and talked to his followers from a dentist's chair.

For the next six years Tim[25] had to wear orange clothes and live in a commune. His mother lived with the other adults, so Yogesh (Tim's new name) had to live with all the other children.[30] Bhagwan thought children didn't need their parents and developed their personality best when they were free. As a[35] result, the kids in the commune didn't have to go to school every day and did what they wanted most of the time. Tim liked the freedom, but he was[40] also very lonely. The kids had to share their parents as well as their toys. Tim had two hundred mothers and fathers, but nobody kissed him goodnight.[45] At night he slept with pieces of Lego – his only possessions.

When he was 10, Tim left the commune[50] and went to live with his father in San Francisco. Not long after this, the police arrested Bhagwhan for[55] fraud and other crimes. Tim went back to England to live with his mother, but for many years he was[60] angry with her. As a teenager, he drank and took a lot of drugs.

Today Tim can see the positive side of his unusual[65] childhood. He even feels he must defend his mother. He says she had to do it: she needed to find a new way of living; she needed to be free.[70]

C   Which sentences are true (**T**) and which are false (**F**)? Correct the false ones.

T/F

1   Bhagwan had very strict rules. ☐
2   The commune's children had a lot of freedom. ☐
3   Tim loved living in the commune. ☐
4   Tim's teenage years were happy ones. ☐
5   Tim hasn't forgiven his mother for his childhood. ☐

D   Discuss these questions with a partner.
1   What do you think about what Tim's mother did?
2   Is it better to share possessions?
3   Do we need to live with our own families?
4   Why do people join communes?

4   LANGUAGE

A   Match the structures in **bold** with the correct descriptions.

1 Tim's mother **needed to** be free.	a) obligation or necessity to do something
2 Tim feels he **must** defend his mother.	
3 The kids **didn't have to** go to school every day.	b) no obligation or necessity
4 Followers of gurus **have to** give up a lot of things.	

B   For **have to** and **must** we use the same past form. Find examples in the article.

WORKBOOK UNIT 9: OBLIGATION AND NECESSITY
MUST, HAVE TO AND NEED TO

5   LISTEN IN   ⑬

A Before you listen, look at the photos. What reasons can you think of to ban these things?

B Listen to the radio interview about laws in different countries. What has each of these places banned?

a) France   b) Halifax, Canada
c) New York, USA   d) Turkmenistan
e) Tokyo

C Listen again and choose the correct words.
1   In Tokyo it's now illegal to use mobile phones in a) trains   b) colleges.
2   People want to make their own a) decisions   b) mistakes.
3   It's about government control, or about a) legal freedom   b) individual freedom.
4   Police arrested a 17-year-old boy because he wore a) perfume b) hair gel.
5   The French a) government b) police ban English words.
6   The president thinks a) clean b) white teeth look much better.

D What do you think about the laws discussed in the radio programme?

6   YOUR TURN TO SPEAK

A Role play
Work in groups. Imagine you are members of the government. Discuss what you would like to ban in your country and why. Choose three things, for example graffiti, school and plastic bags. Tell the rest of the class about your laws.

B Conversation
Work with a partner. Use **Language Bank 15** to talk about:
1   the things you usually have to do, or don't have to do at home.
2   what you need to do today.
3   who makes the rules in your home.

7   YOUR TOPIC

Present two or three of the most important rules or laws of your country, or your college, or place of work. For example, discuss rules about social behaviour, clothes, or the environment. Make notes about:
●   what the rules/laws are
●   why these laws exist
●   what happens if you break the laws
●   your opinion of these laws
Tell your class about the rules or laws you have chosen. Answer their questions.

Gold teeth

Perfume

Feeding pigeons

8 EUROPEAN CITIZENSHIP in English

The EU Quiz

What do you know about the European Union (EU)? Try this quiz. Tick ✓ the correct answer to each question.

1 The European Union is a group of countries working together in:
   a) an economic union.
   b) a political union.
   c) an economic and political union.

2 The EU single market is a group of countries:
   a) which use the same money.
   b) without Customs controls on trade.
   c) without passport controls at borders.

3 Which countries use the European currency (€, euro)?
   a) Portugal
   b) Denmark
   c) Ireland
   d) Poland
   e) France
   f) Britain

4 Who elects the Members of the European Parliament?
   a) all European citizens.
   b) the citizens of the EU member states.
   c) the governments of the EU member states.

Diagram:
- European Commission
  - supervises
  - appoints
  - proposes laws and budgets
- European Parliament
- Council of the European Union
- Citizens
- National Governments
- EU law
- EU budget

5 What does the European Commission do?
   a) proposes new laws.
   b) rejects or passes new laws.
   c) changes laws of EU member states.

6 The motto of the EU is "Unity in diversity". What does it mean?
   a) EU countries keep their national identity but work together.
   b) All EU countries must be the same.
   c) The EU makes all the decisions for each EU country.

A Find words in the quiz which mean:
1 people who live in a country
2 vote for
3 suggest a new law
4 not agree to a law
5 different countries working together

B Complete the sentences with the two words that are missing from each.
1 The ……………… ……………… are the countries in the EU.
2 The ……………… ……………… is the economic region of the EU.
3 The euro is the ……………… ………………
4 People can travel between most EU countries without ……………… or ……………… controls.
5 The European ……………… , the European ……………… and the Council of the European Union make EU laws.

C What do you think? Is it possible to have the same laws for so many different countries? Is it a good idea?

9 PORTFOLIO WRITING

Write a short article for a magazine with the title 'The EU – good idea or bad idea?' Or write a short article about rules at home, or in school or college. What annoys you about them? Why do they exist? (120–150 words).

10 Your answer: WHO NEEDS RULES?

Do rules and laws protect us? Or do they limit our freedom? Are some rules and laws just silly?

 SEE WORKBOOK UNIT 9

Last word:

Can you use all the language items below? Write *Yes*, *No*, or *Almost* against each.

Functions: Expressing obligation and necessity

Language: *must, have to, need to*

Vocabulary: Rules, laws; the European Union

What's new?

Subject:	Future developments
Functions:	Giving and following instructions; informing about and predicting the future
Language:	*will* future for predictions

1 *The BIG question:*

WHAT WILL CHANGE THE WORLD NEXT?

FACT: Thomas J. Watson, the founder of IBM said, "I think there is a world market for about five computers."

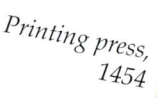
Telephone, 1876

2 FOCUS ON ...

Words

A 1 Look at these pictures of technological inventions. Add five more inventions.

Wheel, about 3,500bc

2 a) With a partner, decide which inventions are the most important. Why?
  b) Which inventions have changed the way we live most?
  c) Which inventions can't you live without?
  Explain your choices to the class.

Printing press, 1454

B 1 Label the picture with the words.

a) switch   b) cable   c) socket   d) plug

2 Put these verbs in the correct sentences.

a) plug in   b) press
c) switch on   d) switch off

1 ...... the TV. There's nothing on now.
2 Can you ...... the DVD player? There's a socket on the wall.
3 It's dark in here. Can you ...... the light, please.
4 ...... the button. It's the red one.

C Match these words from the text on page 47 with the correct definitions.

1 experiment — a) find out if something works
2 laboratory   b) find an answer
3 robot   c) a place where scientists work
4 solve   d) a scientific test
5 test   e) a machine that can do human tasks

D 1 Number these time words in order of size (1=smallest; 8=largest).

a) decade ...   b) century ...   c) year ...
d) minute ...   e) day ...   f) second ...
g) hour ...   h) month ...

Ideas

Discuss the statements:
A The future looks good.
B We have already invented the most important things.

3 READING

A This is an extract from a science fiction story. Look at the picture. What do you think is special about the robot? Read the extract quickly and check your ideas.

It is later in the 21st century and robots work in all areas of life. The Bell family is looking for a new robot to help their old robot in the house. Here, Gavin Bell and his father meet a new type of robot called EGR3 (Eager) for the first time.

They stopped at an old-fashioned house.

"Good evening Mr Bell, good evening Gavin," said a voice.

Gavin jumped. The door opened. 5

"Good to see you again, Peter," said Professor Ogden.

"How did the door see us?" said Gavin.

The professor smiled. "Technology," 10 he said. "Or if you prefer, magic. It's all the same." He took them upstairs to his laboratory.

"I think we can solve your problem," he smiled. 15

"Are you saying you have a robot for us?" asked Mr Bell.

"Precisely," said the professor. "It's rather a ground-breaking experiment. 20 We need to test EGR3 in a safe, friendly environment. Then we'll find out if it can do all the things we think it can."

Mr Bell was puzzled. "Why do 25 you want this new robot to work for us – to do housework and look after children?"

The professor laughed. "Can you remember what robots did in the 30 twentieth century?"

"I know," said Gavin. "They worked in factories, made cars and fridges, those sorts of things."

"Exactly. Do you know how long it 35 took us scientists to build a robot that can see and hear and reason and move around? Decades! But the dream has always been to build a robot that will learn and therefore 40 think for itself."

"And EGR3?" asked Mr Bell.

"It knows nothing," the professor said simply.

"Well," began Mr Bell, "is it quite 45 ready for the outside world?"

His friend smiled. "What I mean is, we haven't taught it anything. EGR3 began life ignorant, just like a baby. Everything it knows, it has 50 learnt for itself."

"But where do we fit in?" said Mr Bell.

When Professor Ogden next spoke, his voice was soft. "We can teach it about the physical world, but we 55 can't teach it about life. Love, fear, anger, …"

"Feelings?"

"But robots don't have feelings, do they Dad?" 65

Mr Bell looked uncomfortable. "You want us to teach …" he began.

Professor Ogden said, "You won't be its teachers. You'll be its family. EGR3 will learn right and wrong just 70 like your children."

A figure appeared and Gavin and his father gasped. Professor Ogden smiled: "Let me introduce you to EGR3." 75

EAGER by Helen Fox, Reproduced by permission of Hodder and Stoughton Ltd

B Read the extract again. Answer the questions.
1 Where are Gavin and Mr Bell?
2 How is Professor Ogden helping the Bells?
3 What can robots do at this time?
4 How did Eager get his information?
6 How will the Bell family help Eager?

C Look at the quotes and answer the questions.

- "Technology," he said. "Or if you prefer, magic. It's all the same."

1 Why does Professor Ogden say that? Do you agree?

- "The dream has always been to build a robot that will learn and therefore think for itself."

2 Are thinking robots a dream, or a nightmare?

4 LANGUAGE

A Look at the words in **bold** in these examples. Do we use the ***will*** future for definite plans and intentions or for predictions?

- EGR3 **will learn** right and wrong just like your children.
- Then **we'll find out** if it can do all the things we think it can.
- You won't be its teachers. **You'll be** its family.

B What is the short form of ***will***? What is the negative form of ***will***?

WORKBOOK UNIT 10: *WILL* FUTURE

5   **LISTEN IN**

A   Before you listen: What appliances and machines do you have in your home? Who uses them? Do you ever have problems with them?

B   Listen to Leo and his father talking. What is the problem? How does Leo solve it?

Flat screen TV

Washing machine

C   Listen again. Who has these opinions – Leo (**L**), his dad (**D**) or both (**B**).

1   Life was simpler in the past. ☐
2   Machines don't save time, they just cause problems. ☐
3   Things will get worse in the future. ☐
4   You can't stop progress. ☐
5   Technology isn't always good. ☐
6   Technology gives us new possibilities. ☐

D   Which of the opinions in C do you agree with?

6   YOUR TURN TO SPEAK

A   Role play

Work with a partner. Choose a household appliance, for example a vacuum cleaner, but don't tell your partner what it is. Use **Language Bank 16** to give your partner instructions about how to use it. Your partner guesses what the machine is.

B   Conversation

Work with a partner. Use **Language Bank 17** to make predictions about:
• the future of the world or your country in the next decade and the next century (population, political changes, scientific developments)
• your future life in ten years' time (your job, where you'll live, your family)

DVD player

7   YOUR TOPIC

Choose a technological development that you think will change the world. Make notes about:
• what it is and how it works
• who developed it and where
• when we will use it
• how it will change the world
• what the benefits will be
• what the possible problems will be

Tell your class about the development you have chosen. Answer their questions. Ask your listeners their opinion of this development.

8 INFORMATION TECHNOLOGY in English

Sony's QRIO playing football

Honda's Asimo giving flowers

A robot's brain is a computer. It switches on the parts of the robot that make it move and do certain tasks. The programmer programs the robot with information for each task. 5 A simple task needs very complicated software and hardware.

The robots of today can talk, play football, walk upstairs, dance and even conduct an orchestra! A lot of 10 robots can see and hear – using cameras and microphones with software that helps them recognise things. Some can even smell. 15 Robots can't think like we do, but some robots can solve problems. 20 They collect information, and process it by comparing it to the data in their program. Then they 'decide' which is the best solution.

Some robots can also communicate with humans 25 at a very simple level: their software can recognise people's body language and how they use their voice. Now a South Korean professor has developed new software using human DNA as a model. He says it will give robots personalities 30 and feelings.

A Find words in the text which mean:
1. computer programs
2. the physical part of a computer
3. to deal with information
4. to give instructions to a computer
5. information

B Are these sentences about robots true (**T**) or false (**F**)? Correct the false ones and discuss the answers.   **T/F**
1. They need the correct hardware and software. ☐
2. They can do many human physical activities. ☐
3. They can think like humans. ☐
4. They can communicate like humans. ☐
5. They have personalities and feelings. ☐

9 PORTFOLIO WRITING

Write an email to a friend and tell him / her about developments in robotics now and in the future. Explain why you think these developments will be good or bad (70–80 words). You can use these phrases to give your opinion:

- I think … / I don't think … because …
- In my opinion, …
- In my view …

10 *Your answer:* WHAT WILL CHANGE THE WORLD NEXT?

What inventions and developments will change our lives and our world? Are you optimistic about the future?

 SEE WORKBOOK UNIT 10

Last word:

Can you use all the language items below? Write *Yes*, *No*, or *Almost* against each.

Functions: Giving and following instructions; informing about and predicting the future

Language: *will* future for predictions

Vocabulary: Inventions, machines and appliances; computers

What's new?

Subject:	Travel and transport
Functions:	Stating the duration of events
Language:	Present perfect with *for* and *since*

1 *The BIG question:*

WILL AIR TRAVEL COST THE EARTH?

FACT: Experts say the number of air passengers will double worldwide over the next fifteen years.

A jumbo jet

2 FOCUS ON ...

Words

A 1 Find as many types of transport as you can for each list.

Land	Sea	Air
• car	• boat	• plane

2 Put the correct prepositions into the sentences.

by	in	off	on	into

a) I never travel …… plane.
b) Get …… the car quickly. It's raining.
c) There was no bus so we went there …… foot.
d) Take the train to London and get …… at Paddington Station.
e) Let's go …… the car – it's quicker.

3 Which forms of transport do you use regularly?

B Match the adjectives with their opposites.

1 cheap
2 dangerous
3 convenient
4 quick
5 eco-friendly
6 stressful

a) inconvenient
b) relaxing
c) expensive
d) polluting
e) safe
f) slow

C What are the advantages and disadvantages of travelling by plane, train, car, or boat? Make notes with a partner using the adjectives above.

D Match these words from the text with the correct definitions.

1 flight
2 fare
3 passenger
4 fuel
5 traffic
6 airlines
7 climate change
8 tax

a) air travel companies
b) planes and cars can't travel without it
c) different weather
d) a journey by plane
e) a person who uses transport
f) the cost of a ticket
g) money that people pay to the government
h) lots of cars or other types of transport

A ferry for cars and passengers

An electric / petrol hybrid car

Ideas

Discuss the statements:

A Air travel is a luxury.

B Quick travel is more important than the environment.

3   READING

A   Read the article quickly. Find five environmental problems that airports and planes cause.

For the last 10 years plane fares have become cheaper and cheaper. Today flights between European cities [5] can cost less than €25. It is easy to book online. For passengers, cheap air travel is a dream and there has been a huge increase in [10] passenger numbers.

But this increase in air traffic brings environmental problems. Aircraft cause terrible air pollution. A [15]

Aircraft pollution

World Health Organisation report has shown that airport noise causes stress and heart problems to people who live nearby. [20]

Airports also destroy the countryside and cause traffic problems on the roads near them.

Environmentalists have [25] been worried about these problems for many years. But we now know about a bigger problem – air travel causes climate change. [30] Planes have become more eco-friendly since the 1960s, but they still produce 600 million tonnes of carbon dioxide each year. [35] Planes cause about 3.5% of global warming today and by 2050 this will be 15%. However, airlines do not pay tax on plane fuel. There [40] are also no laws about how much carbon dioxide planes can produce.

Environmental groups say passengers should [45] think carefully about how often they travel and if their journey is really necessary. Passengers can choose more eco-friendly methods [50] of travel, especially for short journeys. Trains, for example, are three times

Overcrowded airports

more eco-friendly than planes. [55]

Environmental groups also want a tax on plane fuel, or on the carbon dioxide planes produce. But governments don't want to [60] lose their voters. And airlines say they have lost billions since September 11th, 2001. Paying taxes means less money for new [65] technology so that planes can become less polluting.

Air travel is no longer a luxury, but a right for everybody. But are cheap [70] air fares really worth the cost to our environment? Is seeing the world more important than the world [75] itself?

B   Complete the sentences.
1   Plane fares have become … and …….. .
2   There has been a huge …… in flights.
3   Airport noise causes …… and …… .
4   Planes produce 600 million tonnes of …… each year.
5   By 2050 planes will produce 15% of …………. .
6   There is no tax on plane ……
7   ……. want people to think about how they travel.
8   Trains are very …. .

C 1   Do you ever think about the environment when you travel?
2   How can you travel without damaging the environment?

4   LANGUAGE

A   Look at the words in **bold** in these examples. Answer the questions.
- **For the last ten years** plane fares have become cheaper and cheaper.
- Environmentalists have been worried **for many years**.
- Planes have become more eco-friendly **since the 1960s**.
- Airlines have lost billions **since September 11, 2001.**

1   Which word do we use for a period of time?
2   Which word do we use for a starting point in time?

B   Make a list of time expressions which you can use with **for** and expressions you can use with **since**.

WORKBOOK UNIT 11: THE PRESENT PERFECT WITH *FOR* AND *SINCE*

5 LISTEN IN 16

A Before you listen, check the meaning of these words and phrases:

- travel broadens the mind
- to calculate
- So what?
- to plant
- I'm not with you
- celebrities

B Listen to Nick and Angus. Write **N** for what Nick says and **A** for what Angus says.

1 Cheap travel means people can see the world. ☐
2 People have planted millions of trees since they started to worry about global warming. ☐
3 You can calculate on websites how much carbon dioxide your activities produce. ☐
4 Your flight from Edinburgh to London will produce 0,12 tonnes of carbon dioxide. ☐
5 It's the government's job to plant trees. ☐
6 We've waited for years for the government to do something. ☐
7 Celebrities can afford to spend money on trees! I can't. ☐

C What do you think?
1 Does travel really 'broaden the mind'?
2 Are personal tree-planting programmes a good idea?

D 1 Does this fact surprise you?
- Mobile phone chargers waste 95% of the energy they use, because they are on for longer than necessary.
2 In what other ways can we reduce carbon dioxide?

6 YOUR TURN TO SPEAK

A Role play
Your boss often travels by plane for work. You are worried about the environment. Persuade him / her that the tree-planting programme is a good idea.

B Conversation
Work with a partner. Use **Language Bank 18** to talk about:
1 How long you have lived in your town/area and if you are happy there.
2 How long you have been in your English class and what you have learnt.
3 Think of two more questions with "How long …?" to ask your partner.

7 YOUR TOPIC

Talk about a trip you have made recently. Make notes about:
- where and when you went
- if you have been there before
- how you travelled
- what the journey was like
- how your journey has affected the environment
- if you enjoyed the trip

Make a presentation to your class about your trip. Ask the class about their trips.

BIOLOGY *in English*

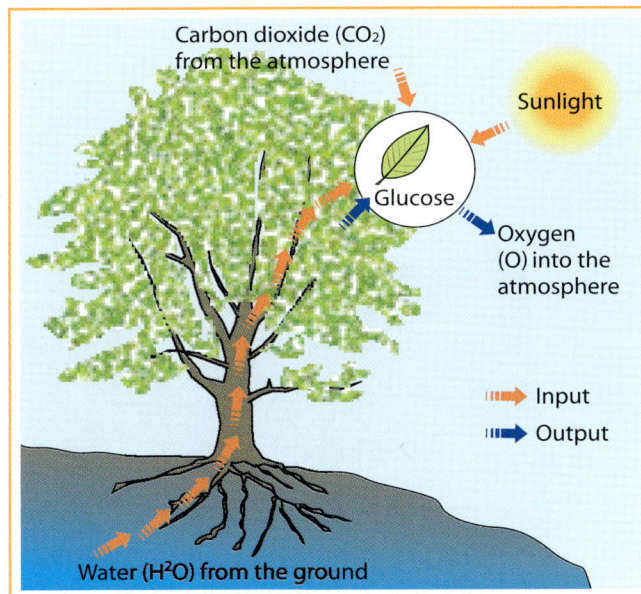

Carbon dioxide (CO_2) from the atmosphere

Sunlight

Glucose

Oxygen (O) into the atmosphere

▶ Input
▶ Output

Water (H^2O) from the ground

Photosynthesis means 'putting together with light'. It takes place in the leaf cells of trees and other plants. Trees take in water through their roots, and carbon dioxide from the air on their leaves. Younger trees take in more carbon dioxide than older trees because they grow more quickly. Sunlight changes carbon dioxide and water into glucose (the sugar that the tree needs to grow) and oxygen. Photosynthesis is the opposite of respiration, or breathing. People and animals take in oxygen from the air and glucose from their food, and breathe out carbon dioxide and water.

Photosynthesis fact
• In one day a tree produces the amount of oxygen a family of four needs to breathe for that day.

A Find words in the text and diagram which mean:
1 the gas that people and animals need to breathe
2 the part of plants that takes in water
3 the flat green parts of a tree
4 a very small part of a living person, animal or plant
5 sugar
6 the power that produces photosynthesis

B Complete the sentences.

1 Photosynthesis:
water + ... + sunlight ➔ glucose + ...

2 Respiration:
oxygen + ... ➔ .... + carbon dioxide

C 1 Why is it a bad idea to cut down trees?
2 Why do young trees make more oxygen than old trees?

9 PORTFOLIO WRITING

Write about the advantages and disadvantages of cheap air travel (120–150 words). Use this paragraph plan:
1 The advantages (speed, cost, chance to see the world)
2 The disadvantages (environmental problems, crowds, noise)
3 If you have flown and your opinion.

10 *Your answer:* WILL AIR TRAVEL COST THE EARTH?

Is cheap air travel a selfish luxury? Are we destroying our planet? Whose job is it to help the environment?

 SEE WORKBOOK UNIT 11

Last word:

Can you use all the language items below? Write *Yes*, *No*, or *Almost* against each.

Functions:	Stating the duration of events
Language:	Present perfect with *for* and *since*
Vocabulary:	Transport and travel; the environment

Money, money, money

What's new?

Subject:	Money
Functions:	Using telephone banking; expressing certainty and uncertainty
Language:	Modals of certainty and uncertainty: *will* and *might*

1 *The BIG question:*

HOW HONEST ARE YOU?

> **FACT:** In a survey 77% of people said honesty was the most important personal quality; 67% of young people aged 15–24 agreed with this.

2 FOCUS ON ...

Words

A 1 Match these banking words with their definitions:

1	notes are	a) a machine that gives out money
2	coins are	b) how the bank keeps your money
3	a cashpoint (an ATM) is	c) metal money
4	a pin number is	d) how much money you have in your account
5	a bank account is	e) paper money
6	your bank balance is	f) your secret number to use a cashpoint (ATM)

B You want to find out your bank balance by phone. Use **Language Bank 19** to role play the situation with your partner.

C Choose three of the words in the box to match the pictures.

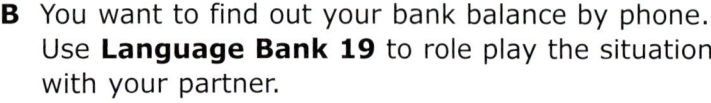

1 beg	2 win	3 earn	4 borrow
5 steal	6 spend	7 save	8 invest

D Choose five other words in the box to complete these sentences.
  a) It's a good idea to .... money in a successful company.
  b) Many people try to .... money in the lottery.
  c) Let's go shopping and .... some money!
  d) I've got a job to .... some money.
  e) I often .... money from my parents.

E Ask and answer these questions with a partner:
  1 Do you use internet banking?
  2 Where do you get your money? Do you have a job? How much do you earn?
  3 What do you spend your money on?
  4 Do you ever borrow or lend money?

Ideas

Discuss these statements with a partner:
A Money is the most important thing in the world.
B Stealing is always a crime.

c croft

3 READING

A Read the two articles quickly. What happens in both articles?
Which story has a happy ending?

1. Super Sunday

The next time you go to the cashpoint, it might be your lucky day. On Sunday, amazed customers in the village of Withington couldn't believe their luck – their cashpoint machine gave them too much money – £20 notes instead of £10 notes!

The news travelled round the village quickly and a huge queue of ₅ customers formed at the bank. "This is fantastic! You don't often get something for nothing," one happy customer smiled. "Hopefully, the bank might not notice the mistake." Another customer said, "I don't feel bad about this. It's not our fault they're giving away free cash!"

According to the bank, the security company that put the bank notes into the machine was responsible ₁₀ for the problem. The bank said it planned to get the lost money back from the security company so the lucky customers kept the extra cash.

2. Crime of chance

Last week Joe Cross, his son Jim and daughter Cherie went to prison. Many of their neighbours will join them there. Their crime? They took out free cash from faulty ATM machines. Because of a problem with software, people in the area got over a million pounds from the machines.

The Cross family got £34,500 in several visits to the machines. Then they bought ₅ themselves a new car and a sofa and booked a holiday. The Crosses' lawyer said it wasn't just their fault; the bank wasn't careful enough. The family couldn't resist the chance of free money. It was "like being a schoolboy in a sweetshop," Joe Cross said. What he did wasn't so bad because it didn't hurt anybody. A lot of people agree with Mr Cross. Many people think that it is less serious to steal from ₁₀ a machine or a big company than to steal from a person. In the same situation, might you do the same thing?

B In which article do these things happen?
Write **1**, **2**, or **B** for both.
1 People got free cash from a machine. ☐
2 The bank's computers were
responsible for the mistake. ☐
3 A security company made a mistake. ☐
4 Lots of people used the faulty
machines. ☐
5 The bank said the customers
could keep the money. ☐
6 The customers went to prison. ☐

C What do you think? Discuss with a partner.
1 Is there a difference between the
people in the two articles?
2 Are the Cross family really criminals?
3 You find an ATM giving out free money.
What do you do?

4 LANGUAGE

A Look at these examples from the text.
Answer the questions.
• It **might** be your lucky day.
• Many of their neighbours **will** join them.

1 In which sentence is it certain that
something will happen?
2 In which sentence is the result
uncertain?

B What type of verb comes after the modals
might and *will*? What are the negative
and interrogative forms of *might*? Find
examples in the texts.

WORKBOOK UNIT 12: *MIGHT* AND *WILL*

5   LISTEN IN

A Do you ever do quizzes in magazines? Do they tell you important things about yourself?

B Do the quiz on the right with a partner. Ask each other the questions.

C Now listen to Leanne and Kirsty. Tick ✓ Leanne's answers to the questions.

D What do you think of Leanne's answers? Are her answers the same as yours? What differences are there? Discuss each question as a class.

QUIZ: *How honest are you?*

		Your partner	Leanne
1	You find a wallet with £30 in the street. Do you:		
	a) take it to the police?	☐	☐
	b) keep it?	☐	☐
2	You have a part-time job in an office. Other people take pens home. Do you:		
	a) think it's dishonest?	☐	☐
	b) do it too?	☐	☐
3	You get too much change in a local shop. Do you:		
	a) give back the extra money?	☐	☐
	b) keep the money?	☐	☐
4	The checkout assistant in a big supermarket gives you £20 instead of £10 change. Do you:		
	a) give back the extra money?	☐	☐
	b) keep the money?	☐	☐
5	Your bank account has £1,000 too much in it. Do you:		
	a) Tell the bank immediately?	☐	☐
	b) Wait and see what happens?	☐	☐

6   YOUR TURN TO SPEAK

A Role play

Your friend hasn't done her maths homework. Another student who is good at maths says she can copy his homework. Your friend asks you if you think it is a good idea. Answer her and explain your reasons.

B Conversation

Work with a partner. Use **Language Bank 20** to ask each other these questions. Explain your answers.

Do you think that:

1   everyone will use internet banking in the future?

2   you'll be a rich investor later in life? Will you invest in houses, or companies or art?

7   YOUR TOPIC

Work in small groups. Make notes about:

- What honesty is
- Examples of honest behaviour
- Examples of dishonest behaviour
- Situations when it might be difficult to be honest
- If you think politicians are honest
- If there are advantages and disadvantages in being honest

Give a talk to another group about honesty. Answer questions from the other group about your list of points. Ask your listeners if they are always honest.

8 MATHS in English

Euro €

Yen ¥

Dollar $

Pound £

Foreign exchange

There are over 190 countries in the world and most countries have their own currency. However, in 1999 the euro (€) replaced other currencies in twelve European countries. Some people think there will be fewer currencies in the future. More countries will use the euro and other countries with weak currencies, for example in Latin America, might introduce the US dollar. Ecuador has already replaced its own money with the US dollar. Despite this, it is unlikely that the number of currencies will decrease greatly.

Exchange rates between the main currencies change every day. So travellers and business people have to be careful when they change money from one currency to another.

Foreign Exchange Rates

Currency name	United Kingdom Pound	Euro	Japanese Yen	US Dollar
United Kingdom Pound	1	0.6873	0.005134	0.5384
Euro	1.4548	1	0.00747	0.7833
Japanese Yen	194.7	133.83	1	104.84
US Dollar	1.857	1.2764	0.009534	1

A Look at the banknotes in the photos.
1 What is the value of each note?
2 Which countries use these notes?

B Look at the currency rates in the foreign exchange chart.
1 How many yen (¥) are there to the US dollar ($)?
2 How many euros (€) are there to the pound (£)?
3 How many US dollars ($) are there to the euro (€)?

C 1 How many pounds do you get for €5?
2 How many yen do you get for $50?
3 How many dollars do you get for £100?

D 1 Do you often change money? What is the current exchange rate of your currency against the dollar? (Check online if you don't know).
2 Your country wants to change its currency to the US dollar. What do you think? Discuss this with your class.

9 PORTFOLIO WRITING

Are you good with money? How do you spend money? Do you borrow or save money? Write your answers as an essay (120–150 words). Divide your essay into at least three paragraphs.

10 Your answer: HOW HONEST ARE YOU?

Are you always honest or does it depend on the situation?

SEE WORKBOOK UNIT 12

Last word:

Can you use all the language items below? Write *Yes*, *No*, or *Almost* against each.

Functions: Using telephone banking; expressing certainty and uncertainty

Language: Modals of certainty and uncertainty: *will* and *might*

Vocabulary: Money; banking and foreign exchange

1 *The BIG question:*

DO CARS RULE OUR LIVES?

FACT: There are over 550 million cars in the world and each year about 40 million more are produced.

2 FOCUS ON ...

Words

A  1 Use the words in the box to label the pictures.

b) steering wheel	c) pedal
d) helmet	e) saddle
f) exhaust pipe	g) handlebars

....

....

....

....

a) wheel

....

....

2 a) Have you got a bike? Can you describe it? When do you use it?
   b) Would you like a car? What is most important about a car?

• It's safe.   • It's fast.   • It's a nice colour.   • It looks cool.

B Match the words with the correct definitions.

1	motorway (UK), freeway (US)	a)	they tell you when to go or stop
2	vehicle	b)	a circle in the road; you drive around it
3	traffic lights	c)	how fast you drive
4	junction	d)	a car or bus, for example
5	roundabout (UK), traffic circle (US)	e)	a wide, fast road
6	traffic jam	f)	a long line of cars
7	speed	h)	when a car crashes into another car
8	accident	g)	where two roads meet

C Complete the sentences with the correct verbs.

a) accelerate   b) brake   c) crash   d) park   e) overtake

1 The car in front of me stopped suddenly. I had to …… hard.
2 It's often difficult to …… the car in the town centre.
3 Be careful or you'll …… into that car!
4 I decided to …… the slow car in front of me.
5 You're driving too slowly. You need to …… to go past that car.

Ideas

Discuss these statements: **A** A car is more than a form of transport.
B A lot of people both love and hate their car.

3 READING

A 1 Read the article quickly. What is *road rage*?
2 Choose one of the headings for each paragraph.

▶ Road rage driver shoots woman
▶ Traffic jams cause stress
▶ Speed kills
▶ Angry drivers use cars as weapons
▶ Military-style vehicles

1

Aggressive driving has been a problem for a long time: driving too close behind another car, overtaking and then moving back in too quickly or braking suddenly to annoy the driver behind. This sort of driving often causes accidents. But now we often read about 'road rage': when a driver uses his or her car like a weapon in order to harm another driver. 5

2

Road rage is mostly a problem among young men, but it can happen to anyone. In the USA, a quiet 40-year-old secretary shot another woman driver because she braked suddenly on the freeway. And in another incident, a pensioner drove over a man's leg after fighting over a parking space. Doctors had to cut the leg off. 10

3

Why do normal drivers become different people behind the steering wheel? One reason is stress. Many people today have to travel a long way to work. There are too many cars on the road and a lot of traffic jams. Even small mistakes by other drivers or cyclists can cause road rage. One man tried to injure a woman driver because he didn't like the sticker on her car! 15, 20

SUVs make some people angry

The result of motorway madness in Britain

4

Some people also think that the design of today's cars contributes to road rage. In the USA, very large sports utility vehicles (called SUVs), which look like military vehicles, are very popular. Over 25% of the new cars that people buy in America are SUVs. People feel safer and more important in them and it is easy to use these scary big cars to frighten other drivers. 25

5

Road rage is a real problem. However, we should remember that a lot more people die in road accidents than in road rage cases. Each year there are 1.2 million road deaths and 50 million injuries worldwide. Road rage can kill – but speed and bad driving are the biggest killers. 30

B Read the article again. Are these sentences true (**T**) or false (**F**)?
T/F
1 Aggressive driving is a new problem. ☐
2 Only young men commit road rage attacks. ☐
3 A lot of drivers become angry because they are stressed. ☐
4 Modern cars are also responsible for road rage. ☐
5 Road rage causes most deaths on the road. ☐

C Discuss these questions with your class.
1 Do you know people who are aggressive drivers? What do they do? Are they only aggressive behind the steering wheel?
2 Can riding bicycles be dangerous? Should not wearing helmets be illegal?
3 How can we make our roads safer? Think of:
  • Driver information (warnings about bad weather, or traffic jams)
  • Technology (better cars and roads)
  • Laws and road rules (speed limits; age of drivers; driving tests)

4 LANGUAGE

A Look at the sentences and answer the question.
  • They brake suddenly **to annoy** the driver behind.
  • A driver uses his car in order **to harm** another driver.
  • Many people today have **to travel** a long way.
  • It is easy to use them **to frighten** other drivers.

In which sentences do we use **to** + infinitive to talk about WHY somebody does something?

WORKBOOK UNIT 13: INFINITIVE OF PURPOSE

🎧 5   LISTEN IN 19

Space for all the family

Freedom of the open road

A You are going to listen to a discussion about cars. Before you listen, look at the photos. Make a list of reasons why you think cars are a good thing ➕.

B Listen to a radio discussion. Who says what? Alex (**A**), Deborah (**D**), Graham (**G**), or Helen (**H**)?
1 You need a car when you've got children. ☐
2 There are too many taxes on cars. ☐
3 Cars make you feel free. ☐
4 Cars take up too much space in our cities. ☐

C Listen again. Choose the correct words.
1 A car is a great way to …
   a) save time   b) get a girlfriend.
2 Bikes are much …
   a) quicker   b) healthier.
3 a) Car parks   b) Parks
   … are good places for children to play.
4 a) Anti-car groups b) Bad roads
   … are making life harder for drivers.

D Make a list of reasons why you think cars are a bad thing ➖.

6   YOUR TURN TO SPEAK

A Role play
You have just passed your driving test. Use **Language Bank 21** and explain to your mum or dad (your partner) why you really need a car.

B Conversation
Work with a partner. Discuss the arguments for and against cars. Decide whether you are for or against a world without cars. Then do a survey in your class. What is the class opinion?

7   YOUR TOPIC

The government wants more people to use bicycles instead of cars. Make notes about:
● The advantages of bikes.
● The disadvantages of bikes.
● How the government can make life difficult for car drivers.
● How the government can encourage people to use bikes.
● Who might be for and who might be against this campaign.
● If you think a government campaign like this is a good idea.
Answer questions from the class about your points. Ask your listeners if they have any other ideas about how to decrease the number of cars on the roads.

PHYSICS *in English*

FASTER THAN THE SPEED OF SOUND

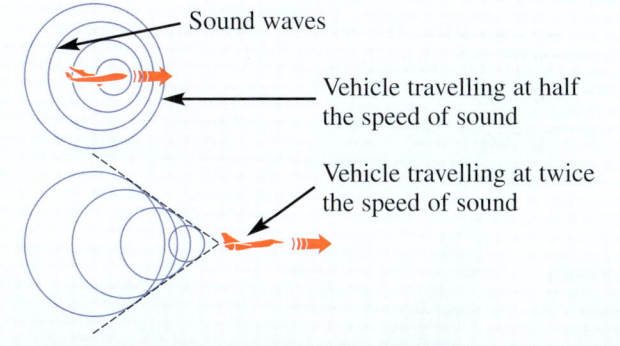

On October 13, 1997 a British jet car, *Thrust SSC*, broke the land speed record. It also set the first supersonic land speed record. The car travelled first at 1,221 kph (759 mph) and then at 1,233 kph (766 mph) – faster than the speed of sound both times.

The speed of sound depends on the weather and the altitude. It is lower ⁵ when temperatures are cooler and also lower at higher altitudes. On October 13, in the Black Rock Desert in Nevada, USA, experts calculated that the speed of sound was 1,196.98 kph (748.111 mph).

When a vehicle such as a jet car moves, it produces sound. The sound waves usually travel faster than the vehicle. When the vehicle travels faster than ¹⁰ the speed of sound, it hits its own sound waves and pushes them back. This produces shockwaves. When the shockwaves reach the ground, they make a sonic boom – a very loud noise like an explosion. People in the Black Rock Desert clearly heard two sonic booms on October 13, 1997.

The jet car
Thrust SSC

Sound waves

Vehicle travelling at half the speed of sound

Vehicle travelling at twice the speed of sound

A Find words and phrases in the text which mean:
1 faster than the speed of sound
2 height above sea level
3 a movement in the air that we hear as a noise
4 a very loud noise when a vehicle goes faster than the speed of sound

B Complete the notes.
1 *Thrust SSC* is a …… car.
2 In 1997 it broke the …… record.
3 It was the first land vehicle to travel faster than …… .
4 It travelled at …… and …… .

C 1 What is special about speed? Why do people want to travel as fast as possible? Is the danger attractive?
2 Would you like to travel in a vehicle like *Thrust SSC*? Why? / Why not?

9 PORTFOLIO WRITING

Imagine you live in a city without cars. Describe it. Think of: the appearance of the city, how people use the streets, what you can hear and smell. Use lots of adjectives to make your description interesting (120–150 words).

10 *Your answer:* DO CARS RULE OUR LIVES?

Do cars change people's personalities? Are cars a great or terrible invention? Do we need them? Are bicycles better? Is speed important?

 SEE WORKBOOK UNIT 13

Last word:

Can you use all the language items below? Write *Yes*, *No*, or *Almost* against each.

Functions: Expressing intention and purpose

Language: Infinitive of purpose

Vocabulary: Cars and bicycles; speed and movement

What's new?

Topic:	Special occasions, family
Functions:	Asking about and describing past activities and events
Language:	Past continuous

1 The BIG question:

FAMILIES – HELL OR HAPPINESS?

FACT: Problems with family members and important life events, such as getting married, are some of the most common causes of stress.

2 FOCUS ON ...

Words

A Put these words in the correct sentences.

1 divorced	2 half-sister	3 stepfather	4 single parent	5 only child

a) I'm an ......, but I always wanted brothers and sisters.
b) I live with my father because my parents are ....
c) It's difficult for a ...... to live alone with a child.
d) Don is Lucy's ...... Her mum got married again.
e) Lucy has got a .... Her mum had a child with her new husband.

B Tell your partner about your family.
- Have you got a big family? • Are you all friendly with each other?
- Which family members are most important to you?

C Match the special occasions with the cards.
1 birthday
2 wedding
3 birth
4 graduation
5 anniversary

a) *b)* *c)* *d)* *e)*

D Ask and answer the questions with a partner.
1 Do you celebrate all these occasions in your country?
2 How do you celebrate? Do you send cards?

E Match these words from the stories on page 63 with the correct definitions.

1	get engaged	a)	a girl who helps the bride at her wedding
2	bridesmaid	b)	a holiday after a wedding
3	witness	c)	a formal celebration after the wedding
4	reception	d)	agree to marry somebody
5	honeymoon	e)	a person who signs the marriage document

Ideas

Discuss these statements with a partner:
A Special occasions are family occasions.
B There are no perfect families.

3   READING

A   Read the article quickly. Choose headings for the stories.

a) *Married in Kenya*   b) *A private occasion*
c) *Traditional wedding*   d) *Underwater wedding*

> **The big day**: Everyone says it's the happiest day of your life. But is it? Two couples told us about their wedding day.

1 ......

Rosie: *I've always wanted a big white wedding in church. Jack and I got engaged two years before, so we could plan everything properly.* 5 *On my wedding day I wore a long white dress and had five bridesmaids. Jack was waiting for me in the church and all my friends and family were* 10 *there too. While I was walking towards Jack, I started to cry. Every time I watch the video, I cry again!*

The reception was in a big hotel. We had a five-course meal and lots of champagne. The speeches went on for three and a half hours! Then there was a disco afterwards with a DJ and everybody danced. 15 *When we left to go to the airport for our honeymoon in Kenya, everyone was really enjoying themselves.*

The wedding cost $40,000. We're still paying for most of it, but it was fantastic to have all our family and friends with us on 20 our big day.*

2 ......

David: *Mel and I knew we didn't want a big wedding. We lived together for two years before the wedding and we wanted it to be our day. Mel's mum and dad are divorced and we didn't want any problems. At first we* 5 *couldn't agree on a place. You can get married anywhere nowadays – while you're skydiving or even underwater! I wanted to get married at the Melbourne cricket ground stadium but Mel wanted Disneyworld. Finally, we chose a* 10 *beach wedding in Hawaii.*

It was really easy. We just booked everything online: wedding, hotel and honeymoon. And it was less expensive than a normal wedding. We didn't want to spend a 15 *lot of money on a party for family members. We don't know most of them very well and we don't like some of them. We got married on the beach in front of the hotel with the wedding planner and a waitress as our* 20 *witnesses. Mel wore a white dress with a bikini under it. The sun was shining on the sea when we said, "I do." It was very romantic.*

B   Who did these things? Write **R and J** for Rosie and Jack, **D and M** for David and Mel, or **X** for neither.

1   paid a lot of money for their wedding ☐
2   got married in Disneyland ☐
3   got married outside ☐
4   did a lot of planning ☐
5   had problems with their parents ☐
6   had music at their reception ☐
7   wore formal clothes ☐
8   already had a home together ☐

C   Ask and answer with a partner.

1   Which wedding was the most romantic? Why?
2   Is it selfish to get married without friends and family?
3   Is marriage important? Why not just live together?

4   LANGUAGE

A   Look at the examples from the text and answer the questions.

- While **I was walking** down the aisle, **I started** to cry.
- When **we left, everyone was really enjoying** themselves.
- The **sun was shining** on the sea when **we said,** "I do".

1   Which of the two activities in each sentence starts first?
2   Are both activities completed actions?

B   Complete the structure rule for the past continuous tense.

I		was		walking	
Subject	+	......	+	verb	+ ......

WORKBOOK UNIT 14: PAST CONTINUOUS

5   LISTEN IN 21

A Look at the photos. You are going to listen to a conversation during preparations for a family party. Before you listen, what do you think is the problem?

B Listen to the conversation. What isn't Mum happy about?

C Listen again and answer these questions:
1   What are Mum and Dad celebrating?
2   What was Dad doing a minute ago?
3   Why was Dad late for his wedding?
4   Who does the painting and decorating in Ken and Miriam's house?
5   Who does the washing at Emma and Andy's house?
6   What jobs does Andy usually do at home?
7   What was Emma doing yesterday evening?
8   What was Dad thinking about?

D What do you think?
1   Do men and women share household jobs nowadays?
2   Have all men become 'New Men'?
3   Who does the housework and cooking in your home?

6   YOUR TURN TO SPEAK

A Role play
Your new boyfriend/girlfriend lives at home with his/her family. The mother does everything for the father and the children. Tell him/her what you think of this situation.

B Conversation
Work with a partner. Use **Language Bank 22** to ask about and describe family activities. Ask these questions:
1   What were you and people in your family doing at 7 o'clock this morning?
2   What were you and your family doing about 8 o'clock yesterday evening?
3   What were you and your family doing last Sunday afternoon?

7   YOUR TOPIC

Talk about a special family occasion you have been to. Use **Language Bank 23** to help you. Make notes about:
* what the occasion was and when it took place
* what the weather was like
* who was there and what they were wearing
* what happened
* what you ate and drank
* if you enjoyed it

Tell your group about the occasion. Answer any questions. Ask your listeners about their special family occasions.

8 THE FAMILY in English

Nuclear family
(two adults and their children)

Extended family *(parents, children, grandparents and other relatives)*

Single-parent *family*
(one parent and children)

Childless couples
(man + woman, man + man, woman + woman)

The family is the most important social group in all societies. However, the family is changing. The nuclear family is still the main type of family, although different types of small families are becoming more common, such as single-parent families. In Britain about a quarter of all families with young children have a single parent, usually the mother. Over half of all UK marriages end in ⁵ divorce, so many people marry again, creating stepfamilies. In some societies, the nuclear family is part of a larger, extended family, which also includes grandparents and other relatives.
Traditionally, extended families worked and lived together. The family educated the children and looked after the old people. In the West, the ¹⁰ number of extended families has become smaller because people now often move to different places. Today, most people have jobs outside the family and children go to school. Friends and work colleagues are sometimes more important than family. Many people choose to be childless.

A Find words and phrases which mean:
1 a group of people who share the same customs.
2 a family with two parents and children.
3 a big family with members of different generations.
4 being without children.
5 a family with children who are not the real children of one parent.

B Are these sentences true (**T**) or false (**F**)? **T/F**
1 All societies have families.
2 The number of extended families in the West is increasing.
3 The function of the family hasn't changed.

C What do you think?
1 What is a typical family?
2 Is a big family better than a small one?
3 Are friends more important to you than your family?
4 What kind of family do you want to have?

9 PORTFOLIO WRITING

Your brother left home yesterday after a family argument. Write an email to your friend and describe what happened (70–80 words).

10 *Your answer:* FAMILIES – HELL OR HAPPINESS?

How important is your family to you? Do you celebrate special events as a family?

See Workbook Unit 14

Last word:

Can you use all the language items below? Write *Yes*, *No*, or *Almost* against each.

Functions: Asking about and describing past activities and events

Language: Past continuous

Vocabulary: Special occasions; family

What's new?

Subject:	Health
Functions:	Talking about facts; expressing and requesting opinions and impressions
Language:	Zero and first conditionals

1 *The BIG question:*

CAN WE STOP DISEASE?

FACT: The world's longest life expectancy is 85 years for women in Japan, and the shortest is 32 years for men in Sierra Leone.

2 FOCUS ON ...

Words:

A Match the photos with the correct words.

- a) aspirin tablet b) cough medicine c) tissues
- d) an injection e) antibiotics

1

B 1 One partner has a problem. The other gives advice. Example:

- I've got a bad cough.
- You should take/have some cough medicine.

2

a) I've got a headache.	d) I feel sick.
b) I've got a terrible cold.	e) My doctor says I have a virus.
c) I don't want to get flu this winter.	f) I have an allergy / hay fever.

2 Ask and answer the questions with a partner.
a) What do you do if you're ill?
b) Have you ever been in hospital? Describe what happened.

3

C Match these words from the text with the correct definitions.

1 disease   a) pass from one person to another
2 epidemic   b) it protects you against diseases
3 harmless   c) an illness
4 spread   d) not serious
5 vaccine   e) when a lot of people have the same disease

D Use these words to complete the sentences.

a) AIDS   b) cancer   c) heart disease

1 …… often kills smokers and overweight people.
2 …… is the number one cause of death in Africa.
3 Too much time in the sun can cause skin …… .

4

Ideas

Discuss these statements with a partner:
A Health is the most important thing in the world.
B If we spend enough money, we can stop disease.

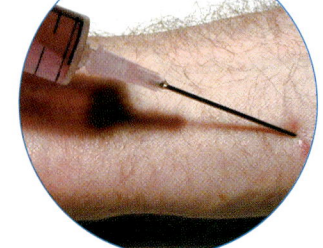

5

3 READING

A Read the Flu FAQs website quickly. Will there be a flu epidemic soon?

B Read the text again. Choose one of the headings for each paragraph.

C Are these sentences true (**T**) or false (**F**)?

1 There is only one sort of flu. ☐
2 Pandemics only affect a few people. ☐
3 Flu pandemics rarely happen. ☐
4 Bird flu is harmless. ☐
5 Vaccines and drugs can prevent diseases spreading. ☐

D Explain these figures from the text.

1	8.3 million	2	1918
3	40 million	4	48 hours

E Discuss these questions.
1 Are you worried about pandemics?
2 What sort of website do you think this FAQ text comes from?

4 LANGUAGE

A Look at these examples from the text and complete the sentences.

Zero conditional	First conditional
• Most people don't worry if they get flu. • If you get a 'type A' flu virus, you can die.	• Unless we do this, humans will get the disease. • Fewer people will die if we develop special vaccines.

1 We use the … conditional to talk about general facts.
2 We use the … conditional for events which will probably happen in the future.

B Complete the structure rules.

Zero conditional	First conditional
• *if/unless* + …; other clause: … or a modal verb	• *if/unless* + …; other clause: … or a modal verb

What is a pandemic?

Will there be another pandemic soon?

How many people die in pandemics?

Can we prevent it?

Can flu kill?

Checking birds for disease

Flu FAQs

1 _____

You have probably had the flu at some point in your life – a high temperature and aches in your arms and legs. Most people don't worry if they get the flu and think it's a fairly harmless sickness. Unfortunately, there are lots of different flu viruses. Many are not very serious, but if you get a 'type A' flu virus, you can die. 5

2 _____

Pandemics are global epidemics where a disease spreads quickly and kills millions of people. Flu pandemics have happened regularly in history: in each century there are about three flu pandemics. In the twentieth century these were in 1918, 1957 and 1968. 10

3 _____

If the virus is a known type and doctors are prepared, fewer people die. The 1918 flu pandemic was the worst in history because people were not prepared. The First World War killed 8.3 million people in four years; the flu pandemic killed 40 million people in less than a year. Healthy young people died less than 48 hours after they caught the disease. Altogether an amazing 25% to 30% of the world's population became sick. The two other flu pandemics in the twentieth century were less serious. The viruses were less dangerous types and doctors prevented many deaths with the help of new drugs and technology. 15 20

4 _____

If we look at the pattern of past pandemics, the next flu pandemic will probably take place in the early twenty-first century. But we don't know exactly when it will take place or how serious it will be. In Asian countries many people have recently become sick with a new type of bird flu, a dangerous flu virus which starts in ducks and chickens and can spread to humans. This might be the start of a new pandemic. 25 30

5 _____

If we take the right action now, we might prevent a pandemic. It is important to kill all birds with bird flu immediately – unless we do this, humans will get the disease. But prevention might not work, so we also need to be prepared for a possible pandemic. Fewer people will die if we develop special vaccines and drugs against the new virus before a pandemic starts. 35

The new epidemics

5 LISTEN IN (23)

A You are going to listen to a conversation between two friends. Before you listen, look at the photo. Why do you think the people are wearing masks?

B Check the meaning of these words.

- to exaggerate
- pneumonia
- hypochondriac
- SARS
- infection

C Listen to the conversation. What's wrong with Jake?

D Listen again. Write **J** for what Jake says and **V** for what Vanessa says.

	V/J
1 If you just feel sorry for yourself, you'll never get better.	☐
2 Think of all the people in the world who really are ill.	☐
3 Everybody's saying there's going to be an epidemic.	☐
4 If you wear a mask, it protects you against infection.	☐
5 Why should we worry about things if they aren't certain?	☐
6 Could you make me a cup of tea?	☐

E With a partner, describe Jake and Helen. Use the pairs of words in the box.

- optimistic
- selfish
- realistic
- pessimistic
- unselfish
- unrealistic

Example:
- I think Jake is pessimistic because ...

6 YOUR TURN TO SPEAK

A Role play
You are worried about bird flu but your friend has never heard of it. Use **Language Bank 24.** Explain to your friend (your partner) what it is, why you are worried and what we can do about it.

B Conversation
Work with a partner. Use **Language Bank 25** and give your opinion about these things.
- people who are always worried about their health
- natural medicine
- big drug companies
- dieting

7 YOUR TOPIC

Tell your class about health and the healthcare system in your country. Make notes about:
- common illnesses and diseases that people have
- what happens if people are ill: free or private healthcare
- the good things about the healthcare system
- the bad things about healthcare
- what you think will happen if there is an epidemic
- your general opinion about health services

Answer questions. Ask your listeners what they think about healthcare in their country.

8   HEALTH AND FITNESS in English

Non-infectious diseases kill more people than infectious diseases everywhere in the world except in Africa. About seventeen million people
5   die of heart disease worldwide each year and twelve million people die of cancer.

Evidence shows that diseases such as cancer and heart disease can be
10 genetic. But healthy living can help prevent disease. Healthy living includes:
- eating a balanced diet
- taking regular exercise
- not smoking
15 - not taking drugs
- drinking alcohol only in small amounts

Did you also know that happiness helps people stay healthy? According to
20 a scientific study, if people are happy in their everyday lives, they have healthier amounts of important body chemicals and a lower heart rate. So a happy family life and learning how to manage
25 your time and enjoy your study or work are good ways to improve your health.

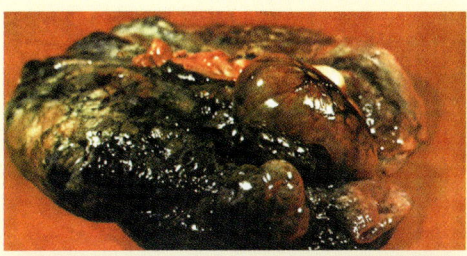

A lung showing the effects of smoking

Smoking: the facts
- Smoking causes about five million deaths a year
- These deaths are easily preventable
- The number of smokers is increasing
- By 2025 every second smoker will die of a disease linked to smoking
- Passive smoking harms other people

A smoker's lung with cancer

A Find words or phrases which mean:
1   can pass to another person
2   to do with the cells in your body
3   healthy food
4   physical activity
5   breathing in smoke from other people's cigarettes

B Answer the questions.
1   Where do infectious diseases kill the most people?
2   What can help prevent non-infectious diseases?
3   Why is happiness important?
4   How many people die from smoking?

C Work with a partner. Look at the healthy living rules and tick the ones that you follow. Have you got a healthy lifestyle? What can you improve?

D Discuss with your class: Why do people smoke if they know smoking can kill?

9   PORTFOLIO WRITING

Write an essay with the title 'Our health'.
Paragraph 1: Describe the general level of health in your country.
Paragraph 2: Explain how you take care of your own health.
Conclusion: Describe what people can do to improve their own health and the health of others (120–150 words).

10   *Your answer:* CAN WE STOP DISEASE?

What diseases should we worry about? What is the best way to stop disease? Is it just a question of money?

SEE WORKBOOK UNIT 15

Last word:

Can you use all the language items below? Write *Yes*, *No*, or *Almost* against each.

Functions: Talking about facts; expressing and requesting opinions and impressions

Language: Zero and first conditional

Vocabulary: Health; illness and disease

Adventures in language

What's new?

Subject:	Seasonal activities, English-speaking world
Functions:	Making arrangements; talking about future arrangements and intentions
Language:	Present continuous for future arrangements

1 *The BIG question:* WHY ARE YOU LEARNING ENGLISH?

FACT: Learning a foreign language broadens the mind. Languages open doors.

2 FOCUS ON ...

Words

A 1 Match the verbs to the correct nouns.

1	do	a)	an activity camp
2	stay	b)	with my friends
3	go on	c)	at home
4	go to	d)	a language course
5	hang out	e)	my younger brother
6	look after	f)	a family holiday

2 Match the photos with three of the phrases.
3 Work with a partner. Ask and answer the question: What are you going to do in the summer holidays?

B 1 Complete the sentences with the correct words or phrases.

accent	examinations	intensive course
motivated	self-access room	

a) I'm doing an .... We have classes for 30 hours a week.
b) I'm really ...... to learn English because you need it for a good job.
c) I have a very good ...... when I speak English.
d) In our ...... there are lots of books, DVDs and CD-ROMs.
e) We're studying very hard for our ....

2 Ask and answer with a partner:
- Why are you learning English? Are you really motivated to learn English?
- How often do you use English outside your classes?

C Match the words from the text with the correct definitions.

1	accommodation	a)	tourist trips
2	a host family	b)	part of
3	a packed lunch	c)	name for the London underground (informal)
4	excursions	d)	a place where you live or stay
5	the tube	e)	a family where you stay as a paying guest
6	included in	f)	food you take with you when you go out

Ideas

Discuss the statements:
A It's impossible to learn English at home by yourself.
B Everybody needs to learn English.

3 READING

A Read the article quickly. Do Jiang Li and Alessandro think their courses are worth the money?

17 English courses: What do you learn?

More than 600,000 students come to study English in the UK every year. That's big business! Like every business, the English language industry has both good and bad sides. Two students on English language courses say what they think of their colleges.

Jiang Li from China

I'm really enjoying my course at the University of Lancashire in Preston. It's expensive but it's worth the money. The lessons are interesting and the teachers are excellent. We do a lot of projects, working in groups and we use computers in the self-access room. In the afternoon we usually have excursions. Tomorrow we're watching a play at the theatre. Preston is a good place because the city centre is quite small and it's easy to get around. Liverpool and Manchester are nearby and there's a lot happening. People here are really friendly – and I love their accent! I think I've learned a lot outside my classes because I use English to talk to lots of different people. I've learned a lot about England, too.
I'm staying in student accommodation on the university campus. I don't feel lonely because there are lots of other language students, like my new friend Kumiko. She's from Japan, so we speak English together and we often go out together in the evening. Tonight, for example, a group of us are going to a club.

Alessandro from Italy

I'm on an intensive course of six hours a day in London with a group of other Italian students. We don't speak much English outside classes. Our class is quite big. The teacher is nice but we just do exercises to prepare for examinations and most of the lessons are quite boring. I'm not very motivated to learn because I could do this in Italy – and it would be a lot cheaper!
I'm staying with a host family – Mr and Mrs James. They're OK, but I think they just look after students for the money. They don't really have time to talk to me. They live quite a long way from the language school, so I have to travel on the tube every day. It's expensive and travel isn't included in the price of the course. I hate British food! I get the same horrible packed lunch every day. Everywhere it's fast food with chips. After school today, I'm going to an Italian café with friends for some real food – slow food, Italian-style! But I love London. It's a really exciting, international city.

B Read the text again. Who (**J**iang Li or **A**lessandro):

J / A

1 is living with other students? ☐
2 has interesting lessons? ☐
3 misses the food at home? ☐
4 is on an intensive course? ☐
5 speaks a lot of English outside class? ☐
6 is doing examination practice? ☐
7 spends a lot of money on travel? ☐
8 goes on trips? ☐

C Discuss these questions.
1 Have you ever done a language course in an English-speaking country? Would you like to do one? Why? / Why not?
2 What things should you check when you choose a language course or language school?

4 LANGUAGE

A Look at the examples from the text and answer the questions.
- I'm really enjoying my course.
- Tomorrow we're watching a play.
- Tonight a group of us are going to a club.
- I'm staying with a host family.
- After school today, I'm going to an Italian café.

1 What is the verb tense in the examples?
2 Which sentences refer to the present? Which sentences refer to the future?

WORKBOOK UNIT 16: PRESENT CONTINUOUS FOR FUTURE ARRANGEMENTS

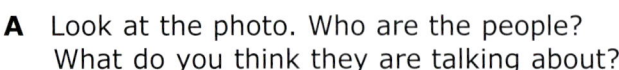

🎧 5 LISTEN IN ㉔

A Look at the photo. Who are the people? What do you think they are talking about?

B Listen to the conversation between Julia, a Spanish student, and her English teacher. What does Julia want to know?

C Listen again and complete these sentences:
1 All …… are different and learn in different ways.
2 It's easier to learn things if I …… .
3 I'm worried about …… mistakes.
4 It's better to speak more and practise …… words.
5 But you don't …… a perfect English accent.
6 There are …… of courses. How can I find a good one?

D How do you learn best? How can people improve their English? Make a list of tips on the board with your class.

E Listen to the last part of the conversation again. What arrangement do Julia and her teacher make?

6 YOUR TURN TO SPEAK

A Role play
Work with a partner. You want to go and see your friend in the summer holidays. Your friend (your partner) has already arranged lots of things for the holidays. Use **Language Bank 26** to help you arrange when and where to meet.

B Conversation
Work with a partner. Use **Language Bank 27** to talk about your arrangements and intentions for this evening and the weekend.

7 YOUR TOPIC

Think about learning English. Make notes about:
• the English language – is it easy or difficult and why?
• which is most important – grammar, vocabulary or pronunciation?
• which you prefer doing – listening, speaking, reading or writing?
• how you like to work – alone, or in pairs or in groups.
• how much you enjoy learning English.
• your plans to improve your English.
Tell your class about your own experience of learning English. Answer any questions.

Adventures in language

8 ENGLISH-SPEAKING WORLD in English

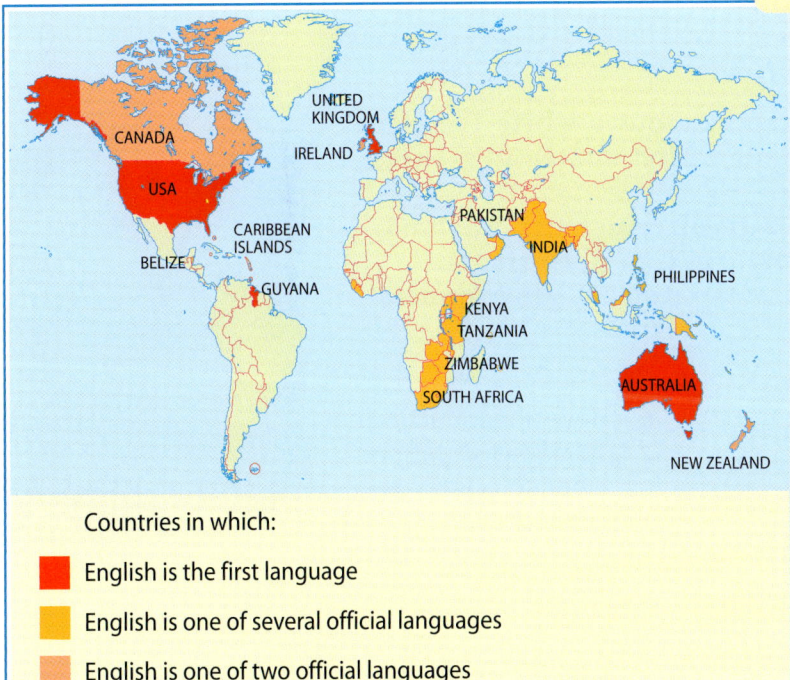

Countries in which:

🟥 English is the first language

🟧 English is one of several official languages

🟧 English is one of two official languages

Facts and figures

- English has official or special status in at least 75 countries.
- Over four hundred million people speak English as a first language.
- More people speak English as a second   5
  language than as a first language.
- About one billion people are learning English as a foreign language.
- The USA does not have an official language but English is the main language of the law.   10
  Three states are officially bilingual: New Mexico (English and Spanish), Louisiana (English and French) and Hawaii (English and Hawaiian).
- The UK has a large number of community   15
  languages because of its large immigrant population. Pupils in London schools speak over 300 languages, for example Bengali, Gujarati, Punjabi and Cantonese.
- The Commonwealth is an association of 53   20
  countries that were British colonies before they became independent countries and where a lot of people speak English.

A Find words or phrases that mean:
1 a language that you don't speak at home but which people around you speak
2 a language (not your own) that you learn at school
3 a language that a large group of immigrants speak
4 speaking two languages

B Look at the map and the text and answer the questions.
1 In which countries is English the main or only official language?
2 Do you know what the other official languages in Canada and New Zealand are?
3 Why can you hear so many different langages in the UK?
4 What is the Commonwealth?

C What do you think?
1 Which English-speaking country would you most like to visit? Why?
2 Is English the most important language in the world? Why or why not?

9 PORTFOLIO WRITING

You are doing a language course in New York. Write an email to a friend and tell him / her about the course (70–80 words).

10 Your answer: WHY ARE YOU LEARNING ENGLISH?

Does everyone need to learn English? Are language courses in English-speaking countries a good way to improve your English? What is the best way to learn English for you?

 SEE WORKBOOK UNIT 16

Last word:

Can you use all the language items below? Write Yes, No, or Almost against each.

Functions: Making arrangements; talking about future arrangements and intentions

Language: Present continuous for future arrangements

Vocabulary: Language learning; the English-speaking world

Extended reading 2

What's new?

Subject: Racism and prejudice

Focus: Reading an extract from a novel

1 *The BIG read:* FACE by Benjamin Zephaniah

The novel *Face* by Benjamin Zephaniah is about a white teenager called Martin. He has a terrible accident which makes him think about prejudice.
Benjamin Zephaniah was born in 1958 in Birmingham, England. He is a poet, novelist, playwright, musician and performance artist. He has also acted in films and presented TV programmes.

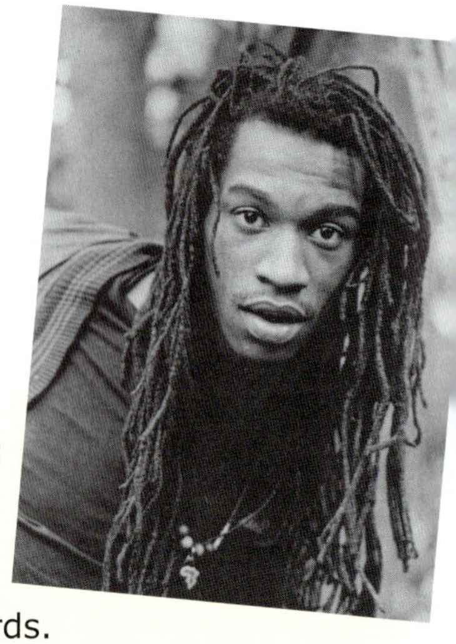

2 READING

A Look at the cover of the book on the opposite page. What do you think has happened to the person?

B Read the extract quickly and answer the questions.
1 Where is Martin?
2 What has happened to him?

C Read the extract again carefully and choose the correct meaning.
1 upbeat a) interesting b) positive c) funny
2 burns a) injuries from a knife b) sports injuries c) injuries from a fire
3 confirm a) help b) show definitely c) not tell
4 survive a) disappear b) grow c) still be there
5 crash a) loud noise b) accident c) situation

D Decide if these statements are true (**T**) or false (**F**). **T / F**
1 Martin has injuries on his face and body. ☐
2 Alan thinks it's a good idea for Martin to look in the mirror now. ☐
3 Martin thinks it might all be a bad dream. ☐
4 Martin was on the way to a club when the accident happened. ☐
5 Martin cries because he is in pain from his injuries. ☐

E How does Martin feel in these situations? Choose one or two words from the box, or use your own words.

angry curious scared
worried determined regretful
upset shocked

1 When he asks the nurse for a mirror.
2 Before he looks in the mirror.
3 When he looks at his face.
4 When he thinks about getting into the car.
5 After looking at his face.

3 YOUR TURN TO SPEAK

Work with a partner or in a small group. Discuss these questions:

A Mark and Matthew are Martin's friends from his gang. Nathalie is his girlfriend. How do you think they react when they see Martin's new face for the first time?

B Do you think Martin will be able to live with his new face?

C 1 How important is physical appearance? Why? What is 'beauty'?
2 The author said he wanted to write a book about racism without black characters. Do you think using a character with facial injuries is a good way to do this?

D Did you enjoy reading this extract? Why/Why not?

Martin's mind began to work quickly. He had now seen the injuries on his body. *Why not his face?*

'Nurse,' he shouted. 5

'Yes, Martin.'

'Can I have a mirror?'

Nurse Ling hesitantly replied, 'Well, it's not as easy as that. The hospital has to be very 10 careful about this. Give me a couple of minutes and I'll see what I can do.' She gave him a warm smile and left the room.

Five minutes later, a man 15 entered the room. He was casually dressed in a shirt and jeans with long black hair which he wore in a ponytail. He looked cool and relaxed. 20

The man smiled. 'Hi, my name's Alan. Just think of me as someone you can talk to if you have any problems.'

Martin was surprised by his confident and **upbeat** nature; he sounded honest and sincere. Martin took a 25 deep breath before speaking. 'I want a mirror, I want to see my face.'

Alan's voice dropped slightly. 'Well, it's a little early for that. Sometimes it helps to prepare yourself, to get used to the idea.' 30

'I … want … a … mirror … now,' Martin said slowly.

'Have you seen someone with facial **burns**?'

'No.'

'When you look in the mirror, you may be quite 35 shocked by what you see. Whatever you see will be improved on in time. But Martin, you must know that you will always have some burns on your face. Your face will never be as it was.'

Martin understood what was being said to him but 40 he still felt that he might just be locked in a nightmare. Although he had seen the damage that had been done to his legs, he knew that seeing his face would **confirm** that this was for real. He was frightened, but he didn't want to show his fear. 'I understand,' he 45 muttered.

Alan stood up. 'Good luck mate.'

For the next fifteen minutes Martin was left alone. Then Nurse Ling and Alan Green re-entered the room. 'Well, mate, here we are.' 50

f a c e

benjamin zephaniah

Alan handed the mirror to Martin, making sure the mirrored side was pointing down.

'There you go. Sometimes 55 it's best to have a glance, look away and then have a longer look. It's up to you, you're in control.'

Martin slowly lifted the 60 mirror up until he was looking into his own eyes. He suffered a silent shock. His eyes were completely red with only bits of white 65 coming through. Then Martin focused his eyes on the skin of his face. It was bright red in places and brown in others. He noticed pinky 70 white bits, which looked like flesh with no skin cover. His whole face had swollen and changed shape. He lifted a hand up to feel his head. Much of the back and sides of his hair had **survived** but the top front had mostly gone, 75 only small patches were left. Martin was scared by what he saw but he could not look away.

Every few seconds different throughts came into his head. *Is that really me? Why me? Maybe it will fall off and my real face will be underneath?* He put the 80 mirror down and closed his eyes. Now he started to feel anger. His mind flashed back to Saturday night, not to the **crash** but to the moment just before he got into the car. He was seeing Pete Mosely's evil smile and hearing his voice saying, 'Come on, let's 85 go riding,' and 'Have wheels, will travel,' and most painfully, 'All right, ya gotta go to bed, we'll just take ya home.'

Martin handed Alan the mirror and simply closed his eyes. It was a clear signal to Alan and the 90 nurse to leave. Martin listened to them go and kept his eyes shut. Now the image of his face was fixed in his mind. Then he opened his eyes and as he did so, he began to cry uncontrollably. He cried for his old face. He cried for his parents. He cried for 95 Nathalie. He cried for Matthew and Mark. He cried for his stupidity. Then he cried for his new face.

Abridged from *Face* by Benjamin Zephaniah, published by Bloomsbury Publishing, 1999.

Key:
Student's Book Page *18*
Workbook Unit *Wu6*
Listening Unit *Au12*

Unit 1

Adrenalin rush
See pages 8-11

adrenalin rush	a sudden feeling of excitement	8
ambulance	a special vehicle for taking people to hospital	11
ankle	where your foot joins your leg	11
athlete	a person who does sport	9
bandage	a long piece of cloth used to protect an injury	11
BMX bike	a bicycle used on rough ground	8
boardster	a person who rides a skateboard or other kind of board	11
bone	bones are the hard bits inside your body	8
broken	past participle of **break**	8
bruise	a purple, grey or greenish mark on the skin after you have hurt yourself	8
bungee jumping	jumping off a high place attached to a long piece of elastic	8
coach	a trainer or adviser	11
compete, to	to take part in competitions	9
compress, to	to put pressure on	11
crack, to	to break	8
cut	a minor injury in which the skin is broken	8
don't panic	stay calm	11
elevate, to	to raise	11
emergency services	the police, fire and ambulance services	11
exercise	physical activity	*Au1*
extreme sports	very dangerous sports	8
First Aid	basic medical help	11
goggles	special glasses to protect your eyes	*Au1*
helmet	a hard hat to protect your head	*Au1*
hobby	something you do for pleasure in your leisure time	8
hospital	a large building where sick people are treated	8
inline skates	skates with one row of wheels; rollerblades	8
instructor	a person who teaches sport	*Au1*
knee pad	something which protects your knee	11
land, to	to come back down to the ground	*Wu1*
motocross	a bicycle used on rough ground; a BMX bike	*Wu1*
parachute	a large piece of cloth that allows you to jump from an aeroplane	*Au1*
protect yourself, to	to keep yourself safe	10
protective suit	clothing that stops you from injuring yourself	*Au1*
race (a bike), to	to ride a bike in a competition	9
ride a wave, to	to surf	9
rider	a person who rides a bike	*Wu1*
roller skates	wheels which can be attached to your shoes	9
scary	frightening	11
skateboarding	riding a board which has wheels attached to it	11
skydiving	jumping from aeroplanes and falling through the air	8
soccer (US)	football	8
sprain, to	to injure a joint (for example your ankle)	8
surfboard	a board used for riding waves	*Wu1*
surfing	riding waves on a board	8
swell up, to	to get bigger	11
thrill	excitement	9
thrilling	very exciting	11
wrist guard	a device used to protect your wrist (where your hand joins your arm)	11

Unit 2

Carnival atmosphere
See pages 12-15

AIDS	a serious disease which destroys the body's ability to protect itself from illnesses	13
amp	a piece of equipment which makes sound louder; an amplifier	15
anti-	against; not in favour of	13
atmosphere	the general feeling in a place	12
band	a pop group	15
beat	the strongest parts of a rhythm	15
cable	a big electric wire	15
Calypso music	a type of music from the West Indies	*Au2*
Caribbean, the	the area between the West Indies, Central America and South America	*Au2*
carnival	a big public festival or party	12
celebrate, to	if you celebrate something, you enjoy it as a special occasion	12
celebration	a special, enjoyable event	12
Christian	a person who believes in Christ	13
clubber	a person who goes to clubs or discos	15
coffee plantation	a farm where coffee is grown	13
commercial	relating to business	13
complain, to	to say that you don't like something or that you think that there is something wrong	13
condom	a rubber contraceptive used to prevent the spread of diseases such as AIDS	13
controversial	if something is controversial, people disagree strongly about it	12
corrupt	not honest; involving illegal activities	12
costume	special clothes	12
creative	a creative activity is one in which new things are made	15
crime	an illegal activity	12
crowd	a lot of people all in one place	14
deck	a piece of equipment on which you play records	15
DJ	a person who plays records at a club or on the radio	15
drugs	chemicals which people take because they enjoy them	12
drunk	if you are drunk, you have had too much alcohol	*Au2*
Easter	the Christian festival which celebrates when Christ came back from the dead	13
enthusiasm	interest and excitement about something	13
feathers	what birds have covering their bodies	12
festival	a celebration	12
float	a specially decorated lorry in a parade	12
headphones	what you put over your ears to listen to music	*Wu2*
hip-hop music	a form of popular music	*Au2*

image	the way something is seen (as good, exciting etc.)	14
Lent	the period before the Christian festival of Easter	13
make a protest, to	to say that you disagree strongly with something	12
mix (music), to	to combine	15
multicultural	involving different nationalities and cultures	12
musical instrument	any object used to make music, such as a guitar or piano	15
needle	the small metal device that touches a record when you play it	15
parade	a big procession	12
Reggae	a form of popular West Indian music	Au2
rhythm	a regular series of strong and weak sounds	15
Roman Catholic Church	the Christian church led by the Pope in Rome	13
safe sex	having sex in a way which prevents the spread of disease	13
samba	a Brazilian form of dance	13
Sambódromo	the street in Rio de Janeiro where you can see the Carnival parade	12
scratch	an unpleasant noise made by moving something sharp across a surface	15
slave	a person who is not free and who is forced to work	12
slavery	to force people to work without paying them and not giving them freedom	12
Soul	a form of music performed mostly by black Americans	Au2
sound system	all the equipment needed to play records or for listening to music	Au2
speaker	the piece of equipment through which the sound comes	Wu2
sponsorship	money given to help pay for something, such as a competition	12
theme	a subject	12
track	an individual piece of music on a record or CD	15
traditional dress	traditional clothes	12
turntable	the circular piece of equipment on which you put a record to play it	15
vinyl disc	a black, plastic record	15
vocal	the part of a recording which is sung	15

Unit 3
Lifestyle choices
See pages 16-19

account executive	in an advertising company, for example a person who looks after individual clients who use the company's services regularly and so have an account with the company	19
accountant	a person who deals with financial records for a company	19
advertisement	an announcement about a job that is free	19
advertising agency	a business that specialises in advertising for others	19

agenda	the list of things to be discussed at a meeting	19
be your own boss, to	to have your own business; to work by yourself	16
boss	the person who is in charge where you work	16
brainstorm	a meeting to create lots of ideas	19
business	an organisation that produces something or provides a service	16
career adviser	a person who gives advice about jobs	18
chairperson	the person who is in charge of a meeting	19
challenging	difficult, but perhaps in an enjoyable way	16
cleaner	a person who cleans in hotels, offices etc.	17
company	an organisation that produces something or provides a service	16
computer programmer	a person who writes computer programs	16
democratic	if something is democratic, everybody is involved	19
employee	a person who works for an organisation or someone else and is paid by them	Wu3
financial analyst	a person who examines the finances of a company	18
financial records	documents relating to money	16
flip chart	a large pad of paper for writing on at a meeting or in a classroom	19
freelance	freelance work is work you do as a self-employed person	18
garden centre	a large shop that specialises in plants and things for the garden	17
geek	a boring person	18
goal	something you want to achieve	Wu3
ICT	Information and Communications Technology; the technology, such as computers and modems, used in communication	19
job satisfaction	being happy in your job and finding it interesting	16
lifestyle	a person's general habits, attitudes and behaviour	16
manager	a person who is responsible for running a business	16
managing director	the person in charge of how a company is run	19
marketing consultant	a person who advises on how to sell products	19
minutes, the	a record of what is discussed at a meeting	19
motivate, to	to encourage you to do something	19
partnership	working with other people or organisations	16
presentation	a formal talk	19
promotion	if you get a promotion, you get a more important job	18
reception	in a hotel, this is where you book rooms and pay	17
reporter	a journalist	18
riskier	more dangerous	16
risky	dangerous	Wu3
routine	things you do regularly	18

run (a company), to	to manage	16
salary	the amount of money you earn in your job every month	18
sales manager	the person in a company who is in charge of selling	19
secure	safe; not financially risky	16
set up, to	to create	16
software	computer programs	16
sole trader	a person who is their own employer and who works alone	16
specialist	a person who has a particular skill or special knowledge	16
survey	a series of questions on a particular subject	16
techie	a person who works with technology, especially in computing	18
training	getting or giving skills and information needed for a job	19
web designer	a person who creates websites	19
work for themselves, to	to work alone, not for another person or company	16

Unit 4 — Stranger than fiction
See pages 20-23

beauty queen	a woman who has won a beauty competition	22
cast, the	all the actors in a film	22
celebrity	a famous person from the world of entertainment	20
challenge	something difficult that the contestants on a reality show have to do	20
character	a person in a story	22
contestant	a person who takes part in a game	20
continuity	the way that things filmed at different times are made to appear the same	23
crew	the technical people involved in making a film	Wu4
critic	a person who writes about programmes	20
documentary	a television programme which gives information about a particular subject	20
dumb (US)	stupid; not intelligent	22
entertainment	anything which is designed to amuse people (TV programmes, theatre etc.)	20
exploit, to	to take advantage of	21
fantasy	a story involving imagined creatures and places	23
fictional	not real; belonging to a story	20
game park	a large area of land where you can see wild animals	Wu4
game show	a television programme such as a quiz	20
gross (US)	disgusting	20
harmless	which doesn't have any bad effects	20
humiliate, to	to make someone feel embarrassed	22
location	the place where a film is made	23
make-over	a make-over changes the way a person or house looks	22
media studies	the study of film, radio, television and newspapers	23
movie	a film	23
news, the	what is happening in the world	20
old man of ..., the	the original ..., which serves as a model	21

plastic surgery	operations to change how a person looks	20
plot	the story of a film or book	23
presenter	the person who introduces a programme	20
producer	the person who is responsible for organising how a programme is made	20
reality show	a kind of television show in which contestants have to do difficult or unpleasant things	20
review	an article about a film, book etc. saying what you think of it	23
scene	part of a film which happens in the same place	23
schedule	a timetable	23
science fiction	stories that take place in the future	23
series	a set of programmes	20
shoot, to	to film	23
soap opera	a regular story about the lives of fictional characters, on TV or radio	20
studio	a building where films are made	23
talk show	a show in which the presenter interviews people	20
they suck! (US)	they're rubbish!	22
trivialize, to	to make something seem unimportant	21
viewer	a person who watches television	20

Unit 5 — Shopaholics
See pages 24-27

account	if you have an account at a store, you buy things there regularly and the store sends you bills	25
afford, to	if you can afford something, you have enough money to buy it	25
bad buy	something that is expensive for what it is	26
bargain	if you say something is a bargain, you don't think it is very expensive	25
billfold (US) / wallet (UK)	where you keep your banknotes	24
cancel, to	if you cancel something such as an order, you stop it	27
cash	money, not credit card or cheque	24
cell phone (US)	a mobile phone	25
cheque (UK) / check (US)	a kind of form that you fill in and use to pay for things	24
complaint	if you have a complaint about something, you are not happy about it	24
confirmation	a statement that something is definite	27
consumer	a person who buys things or uses services	27
credit card	a small plastic card used to pay for things	24
credit card statement	a document which shows details of everything you have bought using your credit card	27
credit note	a piece of paper from a shop which allows you to buy goods for the value written on the note	26
customer	a person who buys goods or services	24
customer service	making sure that your customers are happy	24

delivery	goods that have been ordered, when you receive them	Au5
department store	a large shop which sells lots of different kinds of things (clothes, electrical goods etc.)	24
discount	if you get a discount, you pay less than the normal price for something	25
electronics	computers, digital cameras etc.	24
exchange	changing a damaged article for one that isn't	26
expensive	which costs a lot of money	25
faulty	if something is faulty, there is something wrong with it	24
gift	a present	Au5
good buy	something that is not expensive for what it is; a bargain	26
goods	things that are made and that you can buy	24
handbag (UK) / purse (US)	a bag for carrying your money and other personal items in	24
interest	the extra money you pay when you borrow money or are late paying a bill	25
method	a way of doing something	25
newsagent	a person who sells newspapers and magazines	24
online	on the internet	27
order	a request for goods that you want to buy	27
personal information	details such as your name and account number	27
product	anything that has been made and that you can buy	27
proof	something which shows that something is the case; evidence	27
purse (UK) / wallet (US)	where you keep your cash	24
purse (US) / handbag (UK)	a bag for carrying your money and other personal items in	24
pushy	if someone is pushy, they are a bit aggressive and try to get you to do things that you may not really want to do	24
receipt	a piece of paper which shows that you have paid for something	24
refund	if you get a refund, you get back the money that you paid for something	24
rights	the things to which you are entitled	27
rip someone off, to	to charge someone a lot of money for something	27
rip-off	something which costs more than you think it should	25
sale	in a sale, goods cost less than usual	24
sales assistant	a person who sells things	24
shocking	if you find something shocking, it offends and upsets you	Wu5
shopaholic	a person who loves shopping	24
shopping centre	a large building with lots of different shops inside	26
store card	a kind of credit card which you can use in an individual shop	24
suit, to	if clothes suit you, they look good on you	25
wallet (UK) / billfold (US)	where you keep your banknotes	24

Unit 6

Eat your greens!
See pages 28-31

aubergine	a vegetable with a dark purple skin	Wu6
beans	lentils, baked beans etc.	31
bland	which doesn't have much flavour	28
BSE	an illness that cows got from eating feed made from other cattle; mad cow disease	29
Caesar salad	a kind of mixed salad	30
calorie	a unit of energy in food	31
carrot	a long, thin, orange vegetable	Wu6
category	a type	31
cereal	something you eat for breakfast, such as cornflakes	31
chicken	the meat from a hen	30
chips (UK) / fries (US)	long, thin pieces of fried potato	30
contribute, to	to add	29
crops	plants which are grown for food	Au6
daily	every day	31
decrease, to	to get smaller	Wu6
delicious	a delicious taste is one that you really like	28
dessert	something sweet that you eat at the end of a meal	30
diet	everything you eat	31
eat out, to	to eat at a restaurant	Wu6
export	something which is sold to another country	Wu6
export, to	to sell something to another country	Wu6
fats	things such as butter and margarine	31
food group	a food type	31
fries (US) / chips (UK)	long, thin pieces of fried potato	30
genes	part of a cell in a living thing: genes are responsible for passing on characteristics	30
global warming	the increase in temperature of the earth's atmosphere	28
GM (genetically modified) food	altered scientifically so that some characteristics are changed	30
greens	vegetables	28
healthy	which is good for you	28
heart disease	an illness that stops your heart working properly	28
iron	a metal (Fe)	30
lamb	the meat from sheep	28
leather	the skin of animals used to make shoes, handbags etc.	28
livestock	animals on farms, such as cows and sheep	28
methane	a gas (CH_4)	28
mouthwatering	delicious	28
nutrients	things in food which help you grow and keep you healthy	28
nuts	seeds such as peanuts, walnuts etc.	31
oil	things like olive oil and sunflower oil, used in cooking	31
overweight	too heavy	Wu6
pasta	Italian food such as spaghetti, made from wheat	31
poultry	birds such as chickens and turkeys used for meat	31

produce	anything which is made, especially food	Wu6
research	scientific study	29
research, to	to study in detail in order to discover facts	28
saturated fat	the bad kind of fat found mostly in meat	31
serving	the amount of a food you might eat at one meal; a portion	31
soil	what plants grow in	28
taste	a flavour	28
tasty	which has a lot of flavour	28
unhealthy	which isn't good for you	28
use sparingly	don't use very much	31
vegan	a person who doesn't eat meat or use anything that comes from animals	29
vegetarian	a person who doesn't eat meat	28
vegetarianism	not eating meat	29
vitamins	a kind of nutrient (A, B, C etc.)	30
weight	how heavy you are	31

Unit 7 · **For your eyes only**
See pages 32-35

access	if you have access to something, you can use it	32
blog	a diary on the internet	32
blogger	a person who writes a blog	32
bullet points	dots used to make lists of things	35
chat room	a website where you can exchange ideas	34
communicate, to	to talk to others about something	32
creative writing	writing such as poetry or short stories	35
depressed	very sad	32
diary	a record of what you do every day; the book you write it in	33
editor	a person who corrects what other people have written	32
feedback	comments and reactions	33
flying	travelling by air	Wu7
hates	things that you really don't like	33
imaginary	not real	Wu7
in private	by yourself	32
in public	where you can be seen by other people	33
journalist	a person who writes for a newspaper or magazine	33
keep private, to	if you keep something private, you don't tell it to other people	32
loves	things that you really like	33
nerd	a boring person	34
outline	a plan; the basic ideas and structure of something such as an essay	35
personal experience	things which happen to you	33
piece	a piece of writing; an article	35
post, to	if you post something on a website, you put it on the website	32
private	personal; not for other people	32
professional	if you are a professional journalist, for example, this is your job	33
propose, to	to ask someone to marry you	33
publish, to	to print	33

revise, to	to correct; to rewrite	35
self-centred	a person who is self-centred thinks a lot about themselves and very little about other people	34
self-confidence	feeling sure about what you can do; not shy	32
self-control	not showing your feelings when you are angry or upset	32
self-exposure	showing your feelings to people generally	32
self-help	dealing with your problems yourself, by reading books or talking with people	32, 35
skill	an ability, something you can do	
spot, to	to notice; to see	35
stranger	a person that you don't know	33
tip	a piece of advice; a hint	35
trip	a journey	Wu7
web, the	the internet	33

Unit 8 · **Fashionistas**
See pages 36-39

accessories	things such as belts, hats and bags	36
ask someone out, to	to ask someone on a date, for example to go to the cinema	Au8
baggy	big and loose	36
brand	a make; a label	37
casual	informal	36
checked	with a pattern of squares	36
clothing	clothes	36
comfortable	physically easy to wear and in which you feel good	36
cool	fashionable	36
country-style	an informal style, not smart or professional	37
date, to	to go out with someone	38
designer suit	an expensive, fashionable suit	37
dyed	coloured	37
eco	relating to the environment	37
environment, the	the natural world and the air	39
ethnic	related to the traditions of another race or country	37
express someone's personality, to	to reflect the sort of person you are	36
eye-catching	which you really notice	36
factory	a building where things are made	39
fair trade	making, buying and selling goods without exploiting other people	39
fashion slave	a person who follows fashion very closely	37
fashionista	a person who is really interested in fashion	37
fit well, to	if something fits well, it is the right size	38
flamboyant	eye-catching; very noticeable	36
footwear	shoes, sandals, boots etc.	Wu8
formal	the opposite of relaxed and casual	36
globalisation	the process by which business becomes international	39
Gothic	a style which includes black hair and clothes, and white make-up	37
haute couture	high-quality, expensive fashion	Wu8

'in' look	a fashionable look	37
individual	original; different	37
jewellery	rings, necklaces, watches etc.	36
khaki	a greenish colour, worn by the army	37
latest ..., the	the most recent and fashionable ...	37
leader	a person who doesn't follow others but leads and sets trends	37
logo	the symbol used by a company	37
look	a style	37
loose	not tight	36
luxury	expensive	36
make-up	lipstick, eye shadow etc., which people put on their faces	37
matching	which are the same colour or style	37
military	like they wear in the army	37
model	a person who presents clothes at shows or in the media	Wu8
organic	made without using chemicals	37
outerwear	jackets and coats	Wu8
patterned	with a design; not plain	36
plain	without a design	36
pollution	harmful substances which poison the air, water or sea	39
relaxed	informal	36
role model	a person you admire and imitate	37
second-hand	which used to belong to someone else	37
smart	well-dressed and tidy	36
sportswear	clothes for doing sport	Wu8
spotted	with spots or dots	36
street fashion	fashion for ordinary people, often associated with particular forms of popular music and dance	36
striped	with coloured lines	36
style	a way of dressing	37
suit (men's)	a jacket and trousers	37
suit (women's)	a jacket and skirt	37
supplier	a person or company that provides something	39
sustainable	which can continue without harming the environment	39
tight	too small; which fits too closely	Wu8
trend	a change; a development	36
uncool	not fashionable	Wu8
underwear	knickers, underpants, socks etc.	37
well-dressed	smart	36
wooden	made of wood	37

Extended reading 1

See pages 40-41

break a record, to	if you break a record, you do a particular thing better than anyone else has ever done	40
bucket	a container with a handle, for carrying water etc.	40
deep-sea sport	a sport that you practise a long way from land	41
expanse	a huge area	40
expert	a specialist	40
fame	being famous or well known	40
freeze-dried	preserved by drying at a very low temperature	41
iceberg	a large mass of ice on the sea	41
mechanic	a person who repairs machines	41

meteorologist	a person who is an expert in the weather	40
miss, to	if you miss someone or something, you wish they were there with you	40
nap	a short sleep	41
navigator	a person who finds their way across the sea	41
on board	on a boat or ship	41
rhythm	a pattern; a routine	41
sail	a large piece of cloth used on a boat to make it move	41
sail, to	to travel by boat using sails	40
solo	by yourself	40
soul	the spirit; your feelings	40
voyage	a journey by sea	40
webcam	a camera attached to a computer	41

Unit 9

Rule of law
See pages 42-45

against the law	not legal; which you shouldn't do	42
arrest, to	if the police arrest someone, they stop them because they think the person has done something wrong	42
ban, to	to make something illegal	44
border	the 'line' between two countries	45
break the law, to	to do something illegal	Wu9
citizen	a person who legally belongs to a particular country	45
citizenship	belonging to a particular country	45
commit a crime, to	to do something illegal	42
commune	a community in which people share everything	42
control	the power to decide how something is run	44
Council of the European Union	an EU organisation which promotes unity, human rights and progress	45
crime	something that is against the law	43
criminal	a person who has committed a crime	42
Customs	the organisation that regulates imports and exports	45
defend, to	to argue in support of something	43
drink, to	to take alcohol	43
economic	relating to money, trade and industry	45
EU	the European Union; the European countries which form an economic and political group	45
EU member states	countries which belong to the EU	45
Euro (€)	the money used in the EU	45
European Commission	the EU organisation which makes policy	45
European Parliament	the EU organisation which advises on policy	45
follower	a person who admires and supports someone for their beliefs or ideas	43
fraud	making money by doing something illegal	42
freedom	the possibility to do something; being free	43
graffiti	writing on walls	42

guru	a leader, especially a religious one	43
illegal	against the law	42
individual	personal	44
law, the	all the official rules that are used in a country	42
legal	allowed	44
litter	rubbish, especially paper, on the streets	42
mayor	a person who is elected to represent a town or to run it	Au9
meditate, to	to pray in silence	43
murder	killing someone	42
national identity	what makes the people of one country different from those of another country	45
obey, to	if you obey a rule, you do what it says you should	42
obligation	something you have to do	43
passport control	the check that is made on your passport when you travel to a different country	45
political	relating to power and how a country is governed	45
prison	where criminals are sent as a punishment	42
propose, to	to suggest	45
regulations	rules	42
restriction	something which stops you doing something	42
rule of law, the	obeying the law	42
shoplifting	stealing from shops	42
single market	in a single market, there is free movement of goods, services and people between different countries	45
social behaviour	how people behave in public	44
tax	money that you pay to the government, for example on what you earn or on things you buy	Wu9
trade	buying and selling goods and services	45
union	two or more things which have joined together	45

Unit 10 — What's next?
See pages 46-49

appliance	a device or machine that you use to do a job	48
benefit	an advantage	48
body language	the movements you make that show how you are feeling or what you are thinking	49
brain	the organ in your head that you use to think, and that controls your body	49
button	a switch that you press	46
conduct an orchestra, to	to direct how an orchestra plays	49
connect, to	to attach	Wu10
data	individual bits of information	49
decade	a period of ten years	46
develop, to	to create	49
developments	changes, progress	46
digital camera	an electronic camera that allows you to put photos on your computer	Wu10

dishwasher	a machine for washing dishes (plates, cups etc.)	Au10
DNA	the substance in cells that passes on characteristics to the next generation	49
drive	the part of a computer that reads CDs or other discs	Wu10
DVD player	a machine for watching DVDs	46
environment	a situation	47
experiment	a scientific test	46
fridge	where you store food to keep it cool and fresh; a refrigerator	47
futurist	a person who predicts what is going to happen	Wu10
gadget	a small device	Wu10
go wrong, to	to stop working properly	Au10
ground-breaking	very new and creative	47
hardware	the physical bits of a computer, not the programs	49
household appliance	a device or machine that is used in the house, such as a washing machine	48
housework	jobs in the house such as cleaning, washing and ironing	47
information technology	computing	49
instruction manual	a book that tells you how to use a machine	Au10
instructions	instructions tell you how to do something	48
invent, to	to create	46
invention	a new machine or device that someone has invented	46
laboratory	a place where scientists do tests	46
microphone	a device that picks up sound	49
monitor	a computer screen	Au10
nightmare	a very bad dream; a very bad situation	48
plug in, to	to connect a device to the electricity supply	46
population	the total number of people who live in a place	48
prediction	something that you say is going to happen	47
printer	the machine attached to a computer that makes paper copies of documents	Wu10
printing press	a machine used to print things on paper	46
process (information), to	to analyse	49
programmer	a person who writes computer programs	49
progress	advances; developments	48
robot	a machine that can do some of the jobs that people do	46
robotics	the science of making robots	49
screen	the part of a TV or computer that you watch	Wu10
socket	the device in a wall, with holes, where you connect to the electricity	46
solve, to	to find the answer	46
switch	a button which can generally be on or off	46
switch off, to	to stop the supply of something or a machine; to turn off	46

switch on, to	to start the supply of something or a machine; to turn on	46
test, to	to find out whether something works properly	46
USB port	a socket on a computer for plugging in other devices	Au10
vacuum cleaner	a machine used to clean carpets	48
video	a machine that plays video films	Au10
washing machine	a machine used to wash clothes	48
wireless technology	technology that doesn't use electric cables	Wu10

Unit 11 — Travel costs
See pages 50-53

affect, to	to have an influence on; to change	52
airport	where you go to catch a flight	51
airport tax	a tax that is included in the price of all air tickets	Au11
biology	the study of living things	53
broaden the mind, to	to make you more able to accept different cultures	52
carbon dioxide	a gas (CO_2)	51
cell	one of the very small 'blocks' that make up all living things	53
Channel Tunnel	the tunnel under the sea between England and France	Wu11
charger	a device that refills batteries with electricity	52
climate	general weather patterns, for example hot and dry, cold and wet	Wu11
climate change	changes in weather due to global warming	50
conference	a big meeting where people present research and exchange ideas	Wu11
cost the earth, to	to damage the earth severely; to be very expensive	53
damage	harm	51
desert	an area of land where there is very little or no water	Wu11
double, to	to increase 100%	50
duration	how long something lasts	53
eco-friendly	which doesn't damage the environment	50
energy	power; electricity	52
environmentalist	a person who is concerned about the environment	51
fare	the money you pay for a ticket to travel	50
ferry	a boat that takes passengers on a regular route	50
flight	a journey by plane	50
flown	past participle of **fly**	53
fuel	what vehicles need to run, such as petrol	50
glucose	a type of sugar	53
hybrid car	a car that uses two different sorts of fuel	50
I'm not with you	I don't understand	52
jumbo jet	a very large aeroplane	50
leaf	the small green parts of trees	53
luxury	something that isn't necessary	50
overcrowded	too busy	51
oxygen	a gas (O_2)	53

passenger	a person who is using transport	50
photosynthesis	the process used by plants to create energy	53
plane	an aeroplane	50
pollute, to	to poison	50
programme	planned action	52
Protocol	the written record of an agreement	Wu11
respiration	breathing	53
root	the part of a plant that goes into the ground	53
so what?	an expression meaning that you don't care	52
speed	how fast something moves	53
sunlight	light from the sun	53
traffic	all the cars, or other forms of transport on the road	50
World Health Organisation, the	an international organisation which promotes health	51
worldwide	all around the world	50

Unit 12 — Money, money, money
See pages 54-57

ATM	Automated Telling Machine; a machine from which you can get money	54
bank account	what you keep your money in at a bank	54
bank balance	how much money there is in an account	54
banking	the financial activities that go on in banks	54
banknote	paper money such as a £5 note	57
beg, to	to ask	54
borrow, to	if you borrow something, you have it for a short time and then have to give it back	54
cashpoint	a machine from which you can get money; an ATM	54
change	the money you get back when you pay for something with more money than the thing costs	Wu12
change money, to	to exchange one type of money for another	57
cheat, to	to do something dishonest	Wu12
checkout assistant	the person you pay at a supermarket	56
coin	metal money	54
currency	the money used in a particular country, for example the dollar ($) or pound (£)	57
dishonest	not truthful; telling lies	56
exchange rate	how much two currencies are worth in relation to each other	57
foreign exchange	the system involved in changing money	57
get something for nothing, to	to get something without having to pay anything	55
honest	truthful; not telling lies	54
honesty	being honest; not telling lies	54
internet banking	using the internet to manage your money	54
invest, to	if you invest money, you use it in a way that you hope will increase the amount of money you have	54

investor	a person who invests money in something	56
lottery	a kind of game in which people can win money	54
note	paper money; a banknote	54
opening hours	the times when a bank or shop is open	Wu12
part-time job	a job that is for only part of the day or week	56
pin number	the secret number you need to use a cashpoint	54
quality	a good characteristic	54
save, to	if you save money, you put it away and don't spend it	54
security company	a company which transports large amounts of money for banks and other businesses	55
share	a part of the total value of a company	Wu12
steal, to	to take something that doesn't belong to you	54
value	how much something is worth	57
weak currency	money that isn't worth very much on the foreign exchange	57

Unit 13

Destination disaster
See pages 58-61

accelerate, to	to go faster	58
aggressive	angry and forceful	59
altitude	how high you are above sea level	61
anti-car group	a group of people who are against cars	60
appearance	how something looks	61
attack	an attempt to injure someone or something	59
brake, to	to slow down or stop when you are driving a vehicle	58
car park	a large area or building where you can leave your car	60
crash, to	to bang into another vehicle	58
cycle lane	part of a road which is specially for cyclists	Wu13
cyclist	a person who rides a bicycle	59
drive, to	to go by car	58
driver	a person who drives a car	59
driving test	the test you have to pass before you can drive alone	59
exhaust pipe	the pipe that carries away the gas from a car's engine	58
explosion	a loud bang	61
freeway (US) / motorway (UK)	the fastest, widest type of road	58
garage	a building which is next to or part of a house, where you keep your car	Au13
handlebars	the bit at the front of a bicycle that you hold on to and use to change direction	58
injure, to	to harm	59
junction	where two or more roads meet	58
land speed record	the fastest anyone has ever travelled on land	61
motorway (UK) freeway (US)	the fastest, widest type of road	58
overtake, to	to go past another vehicle	58

parking space	a place to park your car	59
pedal	what you put your feet on in a car or on a bicycle	58
petrol station	where you go for petrol for your car	Au13
pro-car group	a group of people who are in favour of cars	Wu13
road rage	using your vehicle as a weapon; being angry when you are driving	59
roundabout (UK) / traffic circle (US)	a circle where roads meet and that you have to go around	58
saddle	the seat on a bicycle	58
sea level	altitude 0, by the sea	61
shockwave	a wave of high pressure caused by an explosion, or when something goes faster than the speed of sound	61
sonic boom	the bang you hear when something goes faster than the speed of sound	61
sound wave	the wave of energy that you hear as a sound	61
speed limit	the maximum speed you can go legally	59
sports utility vehicle (SUV)	a kind of big car	59
steering wheel	the wheel you use to change direction	58
sticker	a small piece of paper or plastic with writing or a picture on it that you can stick on a window	59
supersonic	faster than the speed of sound	61
traffic circle (US) / roundabout (UK)	a circle where roads meet and that you have to go around	58
traffic jam	a long line of cars that are stopped or moving slowly	58
traffic lights	red, yellow and green lights that tell traffic to stop or go	58
vehicle	a car, bus or lorry	58
weapon	something used to injure people with	59

Unit 14

All in the family
See pages 62-65

aisle	the path down the middle of a church	63
anniversary	a date which marks a special event, for example a wedding	62
best man	a man who helps the man who is getting married	Au14
big day	a very important occasion	63
birth	being born; when a baby arrives	62
bride	a woman who is getting married	63
bridesmaid	a girl or young woman who helps the bride at her wedding	62
champagne	a type of expensive sparkling wine from France	63
childless	without children	65
colleague	a person you work with	65
congratulations!	well done!	Au14
couple	two people who are married or romantically attached	63
custom	a tradition	65
divorced	no longer married	63
educate, to	to teach and bring up	65
extended family	the family including grandparents, aunts and uncles, cousins etc.	65

Term	Definition	Page
five-course meal	a meal with five different parts to it	63
function	what something generally does	65
generation	all the people in a family who are about the same age	65
get engaged, to	to agree to marry someone	62
graduation	the ceremony at which you get a degree, when you finish university	62
guest	a person who has been invited to a meal or party	Wu14
half-sister	if someone is your half-sister, you have the same father or same mother but not both	62
happiness	the feeling of being happy	62
hell	a very bad situation or place	62
honeymoon	a holiday after a wedding	62
household job	a job in the house such as washing or cleaning	64
ironing	making clothes smooth	Wu14
life event	something very important that happens in your life	62
live together, to	to live with someone without being married to them	63
marriage	the act of marrying someone	62
marry, to	to become husband and wife	65
nuclear family	two parents and their children	65
only child	a person who has no brothers or sisters	62
reception	a formal meal or party after a wedding ceremony	62
relative	a member of your family	65
say 'I do', to	to agree to marry someone	63
silver wedding	25th wedding anniversary	Au14
single parent	a man or woman who is bringing up a family alone	62
social	relating to society and how people live	65
society	a culture; a large number of people who live together	65
special occasion	an important day such as a birthday, wedding etc.	62
speech	a formal talk at a celebration	63
stepfamily	when A marries B, if B already has children, B's family becomes the stepfamily of A's original family	65
stepfather	your mother's husband, who is not your father	62
underwater	under the water, for example in the sea	63
washing, the	washing clothes	64
wedding	the ceremony at which you get married	62
wedding day	the day you get married	63
wedding planner	a person who organises weddings for people	63
West, the	the US, Canada and western Europe	65
white wedding	a wedding at which the bride wears a white dress	63
wife	a woman who is married	Wu14
witness	a person who officially watches something happen	62

Unit 15   The new epidemics
See pages 66-69

Term	Definition	Page
ache	a dull pain	67
allergy	a bad reaction to something you eat	66
antibiotics	drugs used to treat infections	66
aspirin	a very common medicine used for pains and high temperatures	66
backache	a pain in your back	Au15
balanced diet	a good diet, which includes everything you need to be healthy	69
bird flu	a form of flu that affects birds, especially hens, ducks and geese	67
cancer	a serious disease in which cells increase in number and form lumps	66, 67
caught	past simple of catch	
chemist	the shop where you go to get your medicines	Wu15
cold	a very common virus	66
cough	an illness that makes you make a noise in your throat or chest	66
dieting	eating less in order to lose weight	68
disease	an illness	66
drug company	a company that makes medicines	68
drugs	medicines	67
epidemic	when a lot of people have the same illness	66
FAQs	Frequently Asked Questions; common questions on a website	67
feel sick, to	to feel unwell in your stomach, as though you are going to vomit	66
flu	influenza; a common illness, especially in winter	66
fresh air	clean air, outside buildings	Au15
genetic	which you can inherit from your parents	69
global	affecting the whole world	67
harmless	not serious	66
hay fever	an allergy to grass or flowers	66
headache	a sore head	66
healthcare	doctors, hospitals and other medical services	68
healthy lifestyle	a way of living that involves exercise and a good diet	69
heart rate	how fast your heart is beating	69
high temperature	a body temperature of more than about 37°C	67
HIV	the infection that develops into AIDS	Wu15
hypochondriac	a person who is always imagining that they are ill	68
infection	a disease caused by bacteria or germs	68
infectious disease	an illness which can be passed easily to other people	69
injection	giving medicine to someone using a needle	66
life expectancy	how long you might live on average	66
lung	one of the two organs in your chest that you use to breathe	69
mask	something you wear over your nose and mouth as protection	68
medicine	something you take when you are ill to make you better	66
natural medicine	forms of medicine that don't use chemicals	68
number one ..., the	the biggest; the most important ...	66
optimistic	positive	68
pandemic	when people all over the world have the same illness	67

passive smoking	breathing in smoke from other people's cigarettes	69
patient	a person who goes to see a doctor or who is in hospital	Wu15
pessimistic	negative	68
physical activity	exercise	69
pneumonia	a serious disease of the lungs	68
prevent, to	to stop something from happening	69
prevention	stopping something from happening	67
private healthcare	health services that you have to pay for	68
realistic	sensible	68
SARS	a very serious disease that stops you breathing properly	68
selfish	thinking about yourself; not caring about others	68
sickness	illness	67
smoker	a person who smokes cigarettes	66
spread, to	to go from one person to another	66
tablet	a small amount of a medicine in a round shape	66
unrealistic	not sensible	68
unselfish	generous; thinking about other people	68
vaccine	a substance to protect you from diseases, given using a needle	66
virus	a kind of illness	66
World War I	the war in Europe, 1914–1918	67

Unit 16

Adventures in language
See pages 70-73

accent	the particular way you pronounce words, because of where you come from	70
activity camp	a holiday centre with a lot of outdoor activities	70
be worth the money, to	if you say that something is worth the money, you don't think it is expensive	71
bilingual	speaking two languages	73
board	a black or white board in a classroom on which you can write	72
club	a nightclub; a disco	71
Commonwealth, the	the United Kingdom and countries that were British colonies	73
community language	the language spoken by a particular group of people	73
English-speaking country	a country where English is the main or official language	73
excursion	a visit to a place of interest	70
fast food	food such as burgers, often to take away	71
hang out, to	to relax	70
host family	a family that provides accommodation	70
immigrant	a person who has come to live in a country from a different country	73
included in	part of	70
intensive course	a course which includes a lot of hours of study	71
motivated	if you are motivated, you will work hard; determined	70
open doors, to	to make more things possible	70

packed lunch	food such as sandwiches, fruit etc. to take with you	70
paying guest	a person who stays with a family and pays	70
play	what you would see at a theatre, performed by actors	71
project	research and writing on a particular topic	71
self-access room	a room with materials or computers that students can use by themselves	70
status	the level of importance of something	73
tube, the	the London Underground	70
university campus	all the buildings of a university, grouped together	71

Extended reading 2
See pages 74-75

burn	an injury from a fire	74
casually dressed	wearing informal clothes	74
confident	sure of yourself; not shy	75
confirm, to	to show or say that something is the case	75
curious	if you are curious about something, you want to know more about it	74
determined	if you are determined, you will make a big effort; motivated	74
facial	on the face	75
flesh	the soft part of your body	75
hesitantly	not quickly; in an embarrassed way	75
mirror	something in which you can see yourself	74
mirrored	which acts like a mirror; which reflects	75
mutter, to	to talk quietly and not clearly	75
novelist	a person who writes novels	74
nurse	a person with medical training who helps look after people who are ill	74
performance artist	a performer who uses various art forms (theatre, dance, music etc.)	74
physical appearance	the way something looks	74
playwright	a person who writes plays	74
ponytail	long hair tied at the back of the head	75
prejudice	an unreasonable dislike, for example not liking people with dark skin	74
racism	believing that some races are not as good as others	74
regretful	having regrets; wishing that something was different	74
scared	frightened	74
shocked	surprised in a bad way	74
stupidity	being stupid; doing something that isn't sensible	75
survive, to	if you survive something, you are still alive after it	74
swollen	past participle of swell; which has got bigger	75
uncontrollably	without being able to stop	75
upbeat	positive	74
upset	unhappy	74